Aeschylus' Prometheus Bound and the Seven Against Thebes • Aeschylus, 525 BC-456 BC

Publisher's Note

Purchase of this book entitles you to a free trial membership in the publisher's book club at www.rarebooksclub.com. (Time limited offer.) Simply enter the barcode number from the back cover onto the membership form on our home page. The book club entitles you to select from millions of books at no additional charge. You can also download a digital copy of this and related books to read on the go. Simply enter the title or subject onto the search form to find them.

Note: This is an historic book. Pages numbers, where present in the text, refer to the first edition of the book and may also be in indexes.

If you have any questions, could you please be so kind as to consult our Frequently Asked Questions page at www.rarebooksclub.com/faqs.cfm? You are also welcome to contact us there.

Publisher: General Books LLC™, Memphis, TN, USA, 2012. ISBN: 9781153804882.

Proofreading: pgdp.net

❈ ❈ ❈ ❈ ❈ ❈ ❈ ❈

ÆSCHYLUS'

PROMETHEUS BOUND

AND THE

SEVEN AGAINST THEBES.

LITERALLY TRANSLATED,
With Critical and Illustrative Notes, by
THEODORE ALOIS BUCKLEY, B. A.

WITH AN INTRODUCTION BY
EDWARD BROOKS, Jr.

PHILADELPHIA:
DAVID McKAY, PUBLISHER,
610 SOUTH WASHINGTON SQUARE.

Copyright, 1897, by David McKay

v

INTRODUCTION.

Æschylus, the first of the great Grecian writers of tragedy, was born at Eleusis, in 525 B.C. He was the son of Euphorion, who was probably a wealthy owner of rich vineyards. The poet's early employment was to watch the grapes and protect them from the ravages of men and other animals, and it is said that this occupation led to the development of his dramatic genius. It is more easy to believe that it was responsible for the development of certain other less admirable qualities of the poet.

His first appearance as a tragic writer was in 499 B.C., and in 484 B.C. he won a prize in the tragic contests. He took part in the battle of Marathon, in 490 B.C., and also fought in the battle of Salamis, in 480 B.C. He visited Sicily twice, and probably spent some time in that country, as the use of many Sicilian words in his later plays would indicate.

There is a curious story related as to his death, which took place at Gela in 456 B.C. It is said that an eagle, mistaking his bald head for a stone, dropped a tortoise upon it in order to break its shell, and that the blow quite killed Æschylus. Too much reliance should not be placed upon this story.

It is not known how many plays the poet wrote, but vi only seven have been preserved to us. That these tragedies contain much that is undramatic is undoubtedly true, but it must be remembered that at the time he wrote, Æschylus found the drama in a very primitive state. The persons represented consisted of but a single actor, who related some narrative of mythological or legendary interest, and a chorus, who relieved the monotony of such a performance by the interspersing of a few songs and dances. To Æschylus belongs the credit of creating the dialogue in the Greek drama by the introduction of a second actor.

In the following pages will be found a translation of two of the poet's greatest compositions, viz., the "Prometheus Chained" and the "Seven Against Thebes." The first of these dramas has been designated "The sublimest poem and simplest tragedy of antiquity," and the second, while probably an earlier work and containing much that is undramatic, presents such a splendid spectacle of true Grecian chivalry that it has been regarded as the equal of anything which the author ever attempted.

The characters represented in the "Prometheus" are Strength, Force, Vulcan, Prometheus, Io, daughter of Inachus, Ocean and Mercury. The play opens with the appearance of Prometheus in company with Strength, Force and Vulcan, who have been bidden to bind Prometheus with adamantine fetters to the lofty cragged rocks of an untrodden Scythian desert, because he has offended Jupiter by stealing fire from heaven and bestowing it upon mortals.

Vulcan is loth to obey the mandates of Jove, but urged on by Strength and Force and the fear of the consequences vii which disobedience will entail, with mighty force drives the wedges into the adamantine rocks and rivets the captive with galling shackles to the ruthless crags.

Prometheus, being bound and left alone, bemoans his fate and relates to the chorus of nymphs the base ingratitude of Jove, who through his counsels having overwhelmed the aged Saturn beneath the murky abyss of Tartarus, now rewards his ally with indignities because he had compassion upon mortals.

Ocean then comes to Prometheus, offering sympathy and counsel, urging him not to utter words thus harsh and whetted, lest Jupiter seated far aloft may hear them and inflict upon him added woes to which his present sufferings will seem but child's play.

Ocean having taken his departure, Prometheus again complains to the chorus and enumerates the boons which he has bestowed upon mankind, with the comment that though he has discovered such inventions for mortals, he has no device whereby he may escape from his present misfortune.

Io, daughter of Inachus, beloved by Jove, but forced, through the jealous hatred of Juno, to make many wanderings, then appears, and beseeches Prometheus to discover to her what time shall be the limit of her sufferings. Prometheus accedes to her request and relates how she shall wander over many lands and seas until she reaches the city of Canopus, at the mouth of the Nile, where she shall bring forth a Jove-begotten child, from whose seed shall finally spring a dauntless warrior renowned in archery, who will liberate Prometheus from his captivity and accomplish the downfall of Jove.

viii Io then resumes her wanderings, and Mercury, sent by Jove, comes to question Prometheus as to the nuptials which he has boasted will accomplish the overthrow of the ruler of the Gods. Him Prometheus reviles with opprobrious epithets, calling him a lackey of the Gods, and refuses to disclose anything concerning the matter on which he questions him. The winged God, replying, threatens him with dire calamities. A tempest will come upon him and overwhelm him with thunderbolts, and a bloodthirsting eagle shall feed upon his liver. Thus saying, he departs, and immediately the earth commences to heave, the noise of thunder is heard, vivid streaks of lightning blaze throughout the sky and a hurricane—the onslaught of Jove—sweeps Prometheus away in its blast.

The "Seven against Thebes" includes in its cast of characters Eteocles, King of Thebes, Antigone and Ismene, Sisters of the King, a Messenger and a Herald. The play opens with the siege of Thebes. Eteocles appears upon the Acropolis in the early morning, and exhorts the citizens to be brave and be not over-dismayed at the rabble of alien besiegers. A messenger arrives and announces the rapid approach of the Argives. Eteocles goes to see that the battlements and the gates are properly manned, and during his absence the chorus of Theban maidens set up a great wail of distress and burst forth with violent lamentations. Eteocles, returning, upbraids them severely for their weakness and bids them begone and raise the sacred auspicious shout of the pæan as an encouragement to the Theban warriors. He then departs to prepare himself and six others to meet in combat the seven chieftains who have come against the city.

ix He soon re-enters, and at the same time comes the messenger from another part of the city with fresh tidings of the foe and the arrangement of the invaders around the walls of the city. By the gate of Prœtus stands the raging Tydeus with his helm of hairy crests and his buckler tricked out with a full moon and a gleaming sky full of stars, against whom Eteocles will marshal the wary son of Astacus, a noble and a modest youth, who detests vain boastings and yet is not a coward.

By the Electron gate is stationed the giant Campaneus, who bears about him the device of a naked man with a gleaming torch in his hands, crying out "I will burn the city." Against him will be pitted the doughty Polyphontes, favored by Diana and other gods.

Against the gate of Neis the mighty Eteoclus is wheeling his foaming steeds, bearing a buckler blazoned with a man in armor treading the steps of a ladder to his foeman's tower. Megareus, the offspring of Creon, is the valiant warrior who will either pay the debt of his nurture to his land or will decorate his father's house with the spoils of the conquered Eteoclus.

The fiery Hippomedon is raging at the gate of Onca Minerva, bearing upon his buckler a Typhon darting forth smoke through his fire-breathing mouth, eager to meet the brave Hyperbius, son of Œnops, who has been selected to check his impetuous onslaught.

At the gate of Boreas the youthful Parthenopæus takes his stand, a fair-faced stripling, upon whose face the youthful down is just making its appearance. Opposed to him stands Actor, a man who is no braggart, but who will not submit to boastful tauntings or permit the rash intruder to batter his way into the city.

x The mighty Amphiarus is waiting at the gate of Homolöis, and in the meantime reproaches his ally, Tydeus, calling him a homicide, and Polynices he rebukes with having brought a mighty armament into his native city. Lasthenes, he of the aged mind but youthful form, is the Thebian who has been chosen to marshal his forces against this invader.

At the seventh gate stands Polynices, brother of Eteocles, bearing a well-wrought shield with a device constructed upon it of a woman leading on a mailed warrior, bringing havoc to his paternal city and desirous of becoming a fratricide. Against him Eteocles will go and face him in person, and leader against leader, brother against brother and foeman against foeman, take his stand.

Eteocles then departs to engage in battle, and soon after the messenger enters to announce that six of the Theban warriors have been successful, but that Polynices and Eteocles have both fallen, slain by each other's hand.

Antigone and Ismene then enter, each bewailing the death of their brothers. A herald interrupts them in the midst of their lamentations to announce to them the decree of the senate, which is that Eteocles, on account of his attachment to his country, though a fratricide, shall be honored with fitting funeral rites, but that Polynices, the would-be overturner of his native city, shall be cast out unburied, a prey to the dogs.

Against this decree Antigone rebels,

and with her final words announces her unalterable intention of burying her brother in spite of the fate which awaits her disobedience to the will of the senate.
11

PROMETHEUS CHAINED.

Prometheus having, by his attention to the wants of men, provoked the anger of Jove, is bound down in a cleft of a rock in a distant desert of Scythia. Here he not only relates the wanderings, but foretells the future lot of Io, and likewise alludes to the fall of Jove's dynasty. Disdaining to explain his meaning to Mercury, he is swept into the abyss amid terrific hurricane and earthquake.

PERSONS REPRESENTED.

Strength.	Chorus of
Force.	Nymphs, daughters of Ocean.
Vulcan.	Io, daughter of Inachus
Prometheus.	Mercury.

Strength, Force, Vulcan, Prometheus.
Strength.
1 21
We are come to a plain, the distant boundary 12 of the earth, to the Scythian track, to an untrodden
2 21
desert. Vulcan, it behooves thee that the mandates, which thy Sire imposed, be thy concern—to bind this daring wretch
3 21
to the lofty-cragged rocks, in fetters of adamantine chains that can not be broken; for he stole and gave to mortals thy honor, the brilliancy of fire [that aids] all arts.
4 22
Hence for such a trespass he must needs give retribution to the gods, that he may be taught to submit to the sovereignty of Jupiter, and to cease from his philanthropic disposition.
Vulcan. Strength and Force, as far as you are concerned, the mandate of Jupiter has now
5 22
its consummation, and there is no farther obstacle. But I have not the courage 13 to bind perforce a kindred god to this weather-beaten ravine. Yet in every way it is necessary for me to take courage for this task; for a dreadful thing it is to disregard
6 22
the directions of the Sire.
7 22
Lofty-scheming son of right-counseling Themis, unwilling shall I rivet thee unwilling in indissoluble shackles to this solitary rock, where nor voice nor form of any one of mortals shalt thou see;
8 22
but slowly scorched by the bright blaze of the sun thou shalt lose the bloom of thy complexion; and to thee joyous shall night in spangled robe
9 22
veil the light; and the sun again disperse the hoar-frost of the morn; and evermore shall the pain of the present evil waste thee; for no one yet born shall release thee. Such fruits hast thou reaped from thy friendly disposition to mankind. For thou, a god, not crouching beneath the wrath of the gods, hast imparted to mortals honors beyond what was right. In requital whereof thou shalt keep sentinel on this cheerless rock, standing erect, sleepless, not bending a knee:
10 22
and many laments and unavailing groans shalt thou utter; for the heart of Jupiter is hard to be entreated; and every one that has newly-acquired power is stern.
14
St. Well, well! Why art thou delaying and vainly commiserating? Why loathest thou not the god that is most hateful to the gods, who has betrayed thy prerogative to mortals?
Vul. Relationship and intimacy are of great power.
St. I grant it—but how is it possible to disobey the Sire's word? Dreadest thou not this the rather?
Vul. Ay truly thou art ever pitiless and full of boldness.
St. For to deplore this wretch is no cure [for him]. But concern not thou thyself vainly with matters that are of no advantage.
Vul. O much detested handicraft!
St. Wherefore loathest thou it! for with the ills now present thy craft in good truth is not at all chargeable.
Vul. For all that, I would that some other had obtained this.
St. Every thing has been achieved except for the gods to rule; for no one is free save Jupiter.
11 22
Vul. I know it—and I have nothing to say against it.
12 22
St. Wilt thou not then bestir thyself to cast fetters about this wretch, that the Sire may not espy thee loitering?
Vul. Ay, and in truth you may see the manacles ready.
15
St. Take them, and with mighty force clench them with the mallet about his hands: rivet him close to the crags.
Vul. This work of ours is speeding to its consummation and loiters not.
St. Smite harder, tighten, slacken at no point, for he hath cunning to find outlets even from impracticable difficulties.
Vul. This arm at all events is fastened inextricably.
St. And now clasp this securely, that he may perceive himself to be a duller contriver than Jupiter.
Vul. Save this [sufferer], no one could with reason find fault with me.
St. Now by main force rivet the ruthless fang of an adamantine wedge right through his breast.
13 22
Vul. Alas! alas! Prometheus, I sigh over thy sufferings.
St. Again thou art hanging back, and sighest thou over the enemies of Jupiter? Look to it, that thou hast not at some time to mourn for thyself.
Vul. Thou beholdest a spectacle ill-sighted to the eye.
St. I behold this wretch receiving his deserts. But fling thou these girths round his sides.
Vul. I must needs do this; urge me not very much.
St. Ay, but I will urge thee, and set thee on too. Move downward, and

strongly link his legs.

Vul. And in truth the task is done with no long toil.

St. With main force now smite the galling fetters, since stern indeed is the inspector of this work.

Vul. Thy tongue sounds in accordance with thy form.

St. Yield thou to softness, but taunt not me with ruthlessness and harshness of temper.

16

Vul. Let us go; since he hath the shackles about his limbs.

St. There now be insolent; and after pillaging the prerogatives of the gods, confer them on creatures of a day. In what will mortals be able to alleviate these agonies of thine? By no true title do the divinities call thee Prometheus; for thou thyself hast need of a Prometheus, by means of which you will slip out of this fate.

14 22

[*Exeunt* Strength *and* Force .

Prometheus. O divine æther, and ye swift-winged breezes, and ye fountains of rivers, and countless dimpling

15 22

of the waves of the deep, and thou earth, mother of all—and to the all-seeing orb of the Sun I appeal; look upon me, what treatment I, a god, am enduring at the hand of the gods! Behold with what indignities mangled I shall have to wrestle through time of years innumerable. Such an ignominious bondage hath the new ruler of the immortals devised against me. Alas! alas! I sigh over the present suffering, and that which is coming on. How, where must a termination of these toils arise? And yet what is it I am saying? I know beforehand all futurity exactly, and no suffering will come upon me unlooked-for. But I needs must bear my doom as easily as may be, knowing as I do, that the might of Necessity can not be resisted.

17

But yet it is not possible for me either to hold my peace, or not to hold my peace touching these my fortunes. For having bestowed boons upon mortals, I am enthralled unhappy in these hardships. And I am he that searched out the source of fire, by stealth borne-off inclosed in a fennel-rod,

16 22

which has shown itself a teacher of every art to mortals, and a great resource. Such then as this is the vengeance that I endure for my trespasses, being riveted in fetters beneath the naked sky.

Hah! what sound, what ineffable odor

17 22

hath been wafted to me, emanating from a god, or from mortal, or of some intermediate nature? Has there come anyone to the remote rock as a spectator of my sufferings, or with what intent!

18 22

Behold me an ill-fated god in durance, the foe of Jupiter, him that hath incurred the detestation of all the gods who frequent the court of Jupiter, by reason of my excessive friendliness to mortals. Alas! alas! what can this hasty motion of birds be which I again hear hard by me? The air too is whistling faintly with the whirrings of pinions. Every thing that approaches is to me an object of dread.

Chorus. Dread thou nothing; for this is a friendly band that has come with the fleet rivalry of their pinions to this 18 rock, after prevailing with difficulty on the mind of our father. And the swiftly-wafting breezes escorted me; for the echo of the clang of steel pierced to the recess of our grots, and banished my demure-looking reserve; and I sped without my sandals in my winged chariot.

Pr. Alas! alas! ye offspring of prolific Thetys, and daughters of Ocean your sire, who rolls around the whole earth in his unslumbering stream; look upon me, see clasped in what bonds I shall keep an unenviable watch on the topmost crags of this ravine.

Ch. I see, Prometheus: and a fearful mist full of tears darts over mine eyes, as I looked on thy frame withering on the rocks

19 22

in these galling adamantine fetters: for new pilots are the masters of Olympus; and Jove, contrary to right, lords it with new laws, and things aforetime had in reverence he is obliterating.

Pr. Oh would that he had sent me beneath the earth, and below into the boundless Tartarus of Hades that receives the dead, after savagely securing me in indissoluble bonds, so that no god at any time, nor any other being, had exulted in this my doom. Whereas now, hapless one, I, the sport of the winds, suffer pangs that gladden my foes.

Ch. Who of the gods is so hard-hearted as that these things should be grateful to him? Who is there that sympathizes not with thy sufferings, Jove excepted? He, indeed, in his wrath, assuming an inflexible temper, is evermore oppressing the celestial race! nor will he cease before that either he shall have sated his heart, or some one by some stratagem shall have seized upon his sovereignty that will be no easy prize.

19

Pr. In truth hereafter the president of the immortals 20 shall have need of me, albeit that I am ignominiously suffering in stubborn shackles, to discover to him the new plot by which he is to be despoiled of his sceptre and his honors. But neither shall he win me by the honey-tongued charms of persuasion; nor will I at any time, crouching beneath his stern threats, divulge this matter, before he shall have released me from my cruel bonds, and shall be willing to yield me retribution for this outrage.

Ch. Thou indeed both art bold, and yieldest nought to thy bitter calamities, but art over free in thy language. But piercing terror is worrying my soul; for I fear for thy fortunes. How, when will it be thy destiny to make the haven and see the end of these thy sufferings? for the son of Saturn has manners that supplication cannot reach, and an inexorable heart.

Pr. I know that Jupiter is harsh, and keeps justice to himself; but for all that he shall hereafter be softened in purpose, when he shall be crushed in this way; and, after calming his unyielding temper with eagerness will he hereafter come into league and friendship with me that will eagerly [welcome him].

Ch. Unfold and speak out to us the whole story, from what accusation has Jupiter seized thee, and is thus disgracefully and bitterly tormenting thee. Inform us, if thou be in no respect hurt by the recital.

Pr. Painful indeed are these things for me to tell, and painful too for me to hold my peace, and in every way grievous. As soon as the divinities began discord, and a feud was stirred up among them with one another—one 20 party 21 wishing to eject Saturn from his throne, in order forsooth that Jupiter might be king, and others expediting the reverse, that Jupiter might at no time rule over the gods: then I, when I gave the best advice, was not able to prevail upon the Titans, children of Uranus and Terra; but they, contemning in their stout spirits wily schemes, fancied that without any trouble, and by dint of main force, they were to win the sovereignty. But it was not once only that my mother Themis, and Terra, a single person with many titles, had forewarned me of the way in which the future would be accomplished; how it was destined, that, not by main force, nor by the strong hand, but by craft the victors should prevail. When, however, I explained such points in discourse, they deigned not to pay me any regard at all. Of the plans which then presented themselves to me, the best appeared that I should take my mother and promptly side with Jupiter, who was right willing [to receive us]. And 'tis by means of my counsels that the murky abyss of Tartarus overwhelms the antique Saturn, allies and all. After thus being assisted by me, the tyrant of the gods hath recompensed me with this foul recompense. For somehow this malady attaches to tyranny, not to put confidence in its friends. But for your inquiries upon what charge is it that he outrages me, this I will make clear. As soon as he has established himself on his father's throne, he assigns forthwith to the different divinities each his honors, and he was marshaling in order his empire; but of woe-begone mortals he made no account, but wished, after 21 having annihilated the entire race, to plant another new one. And these schemes no one opposed except myself: But I dared: I ransomed mortals from being utterly destroyed, and going down to Hades. 'Tis for this, in truth, that I am bent by sufferings such as these, agonizing to endure, and piteous to look upon. I that had compassion for mortals, have myself been deemed unworthy to obtain this, but mercilessly am thus coerced to order, a spectacle inglorious to Jupiter.

Ch. Iron-hearted and formed of rock too, Prometheus, is he, who condoles not with thy toils: for I could have wished never to have beheld them, and now, when I behold them, I am pained in my heart.

Pr. Ay, in very deed I am a piteous object for friends to behold.

Ch. And didst thou chance to advance even beyond this?

Pr. Yes! I prevented mortals from foreseeing their doom.

Ch. By finding what remedy for this malady?

Pr. I caused blind hopes to dwell within them.

Ch. In this thou gavest a mighty benefit to mortals.

Pr. Over and above these boons, however, I imparted fire to them.

Ch. And do the creatures of a day now possess bright fire?

Pr. Yes—from which they will moreover learn thoroughly many arts.

Ch. Is it indeed on charges such as these that Jupiter is both visiting thee with indignities, and in no wise grants thee a respite from thy pains? And is no period to thy toils set before thee?

Pr. None other assuredly, but when it may please him.

Ch. And how shall it be his good pleasure? What hope is there? Seest thou not that thou didst err? but how thou 22 didst err, I can not relate with pleasure, and it would be a pain to you. But let us leave these points, and search thou for some escape from thine agony.

Pr. 'Tis easy, for any one that hath his foot unentangled by sufferings, both to exhort and to admonish him that is in evil plight. But I knew all these things willingly, willingly I erred, I will not gainsay it; and in doing service to mortals I brought upon myself sufferings. Yet not at all did I imagine, that, in such a punishment as this, I was to wither away upon lofty rocks, meeting with this desolate solitary crag. And yet wail ye not over my present sorrows, but after alighting on the ground, list ye to the fortune that is coming on, that ye may learn the whole throughout. Yield to me, yield ye, take ye a share in the woes of him that is now suffering. Hence in the same way doth calamity, roaming to and fro, settle down on different individuals.

Ch. Upon those who are nothing loth hast thou urged this, Prometheus: and now having with light step quitted my rapidly-wafted chariot-seat, and the pure æther, highway of the feathered race, I will draw near to this rugged ground: and I long to hear the whole tale of thy sufferings.

Enter Ocean .

I am arrived at the end of a long journey, 22 having passed over [it] to thee, Prometheus, guiding this winged steed of mine, swift of pinion, by my will, without a bit; and, rest assured, I sorrow with thy misfortunes. For both the tie of kindred thus constrains me, and, relationship apart, there is no one on whom I would bestow a larger share [of my regard] than to thyself. And thou shalt know that these words are sincere, and that it is not in me vainly to do lip-service; for come, signify to me in what it is necessary for 23 me to assist thee; for at no time shalt thou say that thou hast a stancher friend than Oceanus.

Pr. Hah! what means this? and hast thou too come to be a witness of my pangs? How hast thou ventured, after quitting both the stream that bears thy name, and the rock-roofed self-wrought 23 grots, to come into the iron teeming land? Is it that you may contemplate my misfortunes, and as sympathizing with my woes that thou hast come? Behold a spectacle, me here the friend of Jupiter, that helped to establish his sovereignty, with what pains I am bent by him.

Oc. I see, Prometheus, and to thee, subtle as thou art, I wish to give the best counsel. Know thyself, and assume to thyself new manners; for among the gods too there is a new monarch. But if thou wilt utter words thus harsh and whetted, Jupiter mayhap, though seated far aloft, will hear thee, so that the present bitterness of sufferings will seem to thee to be child's play. But, O hapless one! dismiss the passion which thou feelest, and search for a deliverance from these sufferings of thine. Old-fashioned maxims these, it may be, I appear to thee to utter; yet such becomes the wages of the tongue that talks too proudly. But not even yet art thou humble, nor submittest to ills; and in addition to those that already beset thee, thou art willing to bring others upon thee. Yet not, if at least thou takest me for thy instructor, 24 wilt thou stretch out thy leg against the pricks; as thou seest that a harsh monarch, and one that is not subject to control, is lording it. And now I for my part will go, and will essay, if I be able, to disinthrall thee from these thy pangs. But be thou still, nor be over impetuous in thy language. What! knowest thou not exactly, extremely intelligent as thou art, that punishment is inflicted on a froward tongue?

Pr. I give thee joy, because that thou hast escaped censure, after taking part in and venturing along with me in all things. And now leave him alone, and let it not concern thee. For in no wise wilt thou persuade him; for he is not open to persuasion. And look thou well to it that thou take not harm thyself by the journey.

Oc. Thou art far better calculated by nature to instruct thy neighbors than thyself: I draw my conclusion from fact, and not from word. But think not for a moment to divert me from the attempt. For I am confident, yea, I am confident, that Jupiter will grant me this boon, so as to release thee from these pangs of thine.

Pr. In part I commend thee, and will by no means at any time cease to do so. For in zeal to serve me thou lackest nothing. But trouble thyself not; for in vain, without being of any service to me, 24 wilt thou labor, if in any respect thou art willing to labor. But hold thou thy peace, and keep thyself out of harm's way; for I, though I be in misfortune, would not on this account be willing that sufferings 25 should befall as many as possible. No, indeed, since also the disasters of my brother Atlas gall my heart, who is stationed in the western regions, sustaining on his shoulders the pillar of heaven and of earth, a burden not of easy grasp. I commiserated too when I beheld the earth-born inmate of the Cilician caverns, a tremendous prodigy, the hundred-headed impetuous Typhon, overpowered by force, who withstood all the gods, hissing slaughter from his hungry jaws; and from his eyes there flashed a hideous glare, as though he would perforce overthrow the sovereignty of Jove. But the sleepless shaft of Jupiter came upon him, the descending thunderbolt breathing forth flame, which scared him out of his presumptuous bravadoes; for having been smitten to his very soul he was crumbled to a cinder, and thunder-blasted in his prowess. And now, a helpless and paralyzed form is he lying hard by a narrow frith, pressed down beneath the roots of Ætna. 25 And, seated on the topmost peaks, Vulcan 26 forges the molten masses, whence there shall one day burst forth floods devouring with fell jaws the level fields of fruitful Sicily: with rage such as this shall Typhon boil over in hot artillery of a never-glutted fire-breathing storm; albeit he hath been reduced to ashes by the thunder-bolt of Jupiter. But thou art no novice, nor needest thou me for thine instructor. Save thyself as best thou knowest how; but I will exhaust my present fate until such time as the spirit of Jupiter shall abate its wrath.

Oc. Knowest thou not this then, Prometheus, that words are the physicians of a distempered feeling? 26

Pr. True, if one seasonably soften down the heart, and do not with rude violence reduce a swelling spirit.

Oc. Ay, but in foresight along with boldness 27 what mischief is there that thou seest to be inherent? inform me.

Pr. Superfluous trouble and trifling folly.

Oc. Suffer me to sicken in this said sickness, since 'tis of the highest advantage for one that is wise not to seem to be wise.

Pr. (Not so, for) this trespass will seem to be mine.

27

Oc. Thy language is plainly sending me back to my home.

Pr. Lest thy lamentation over me bring thee into ill-will.

Oc. What with him who hath lately seated himself on the throne that ruleth over all?

Pr. Beware of him lest at any time his heart be moved to wrath.

Oc. Thy disaster, Prometheus, is my monitor.

Pr. Away! withdraw thee, keep thy present determination.

Oc. On me, hastening to start, hast thou urged this injunction; for my winged quadruped flaps with his pinions the smooth track of æther; and blithely would he recline his limbs in his stalls at home.

[*Exit* Ocean.

Ch. I bewail thee for thy lost fate, Prometheus. A flood of trickling tears from my yielding eyes has bedewed my cheek with its humid gushings; for Jupiter commanding this thine unenviable doom by laws of his own, displays his spear appearing superior o'er the gods of old. 28 And now the whole land echoes with wailing—they wail thy stately and time-graced honors, and those of thy brethren; and all they of mortal race that occupy a dwelling neighboring on hallowed Asia 29 mourn with thy deeply-deplorable sufferings: the virgins that dwell in the land of Colchis too, fearless of the fight, and the Scythian horde who possess the most remote regions of earth around lake Mæotis; and the war-like flower of Arabia, 30 who occupy a fortress on the craggy 28 heights in the neighborhood of Caucasus, a warrior-host, clamoring amid sharply-barbed spears.

One other god only, indeed, have I heretofore beheld in miseries, the Titan Atlas, subdued by the galling of adamantine 31 bonds, who evermore in his back is groaning beneath 32 the excessive mighty mass of the pole of heaven. And the billow of the deep roars as it falls in cadence, the depth moans, and the murky vault of Hades rumbles beneath the earth, and the fountains of the pure streaming rivers wail for his piteous pains.

Pr. Do not, I pray you, suppose that I am holding my peace from pride or self-will; but by reflection am I gnawed to the heart, seeing myself thus ignominiously entreated. 33 And yet who but myself defined completely the prerogative for these same new gods? But on these matters I say nothing, for I should speak to you already acquainted with these things. But for the misfortunes that existed among mortals, hear how I made them, that aforetime lived as infants, rational and possessed of intellect. 34 And I will tell you, 29 having no complaint against mankind, as detailing the kindness of the boons which I bestowed upon them: they who at first seeing saw in vain, hearing they heard not. But, like to the forms of dreams, for a long time they used to huddle together all things at random, and naught knew they about brick-built 35 and sun-ward houses, nor carpentry; but they dwelt in the excavated earth like tiny emmets in the sunless depths of caverns. And they had no sure sign either of winter, or of flowery spring, or of fruitful summer; but they used to do every thing without judgment, until indeed I showed to them the risings of the stars and their settings, 36 hard to be discerned.

And verily I discover for them Numbers, the surpassing all inventions, 37 the combinations too of letters, and Memory, 30 effective mother-nurse of all arts. I also first bound with yokes beasts submissive to the collars; and in order that with their bodies they might become to mortals substitutes for their severest toils, I brought steeds under cars obedient to the rein, 38 a glory to pompous luxury. And none other than I invented the canvas-winged chariots of mariners that roam over the ocean. After discovering for mortals such inventions, wretch that I am, I myself have no device whereby I may escape from my present misery.

Ch. Thou hast suffered unseemly ills, baulked in thy discretion thou art erring; and like a bad physician, having fallen into a distemper thou art faint-hearted, and, in reference to thyself, thou canst not discover by what manner of medicines thou mayest be cured.

Pr. When thou hearest the rest of my tale, thou wilt wonder still more what arts and resources I contrived. For the greatest—if that any one fell into a distemper, there was no remedy, neither in the way of diet, nor of liniment, nor of potion, but for lack of medicines they used to pine away to skeletons, before that I pointed out to them the composition 39 of mild remedies, wherewith they ward off all their maladies. Many modes too of the divining art did I classify, and was the first that discriminated among dreams those which are destined to be a true vision; obscure vocal omens 40 too I made 31 known to them; tokens also incidental on the road, and the flight of birds of crooked talons I clearly defined, both those that are in their nature auspicious, and the ill-omened, and what the kind of life that each leads, and what are their feuds and endearments 41 and intercourse one with another: the smoothness too of the entrails, and what hue they must have to be acceptable to the gods, the various happy formations of the gall and liver, and the limbs enveloped in fat: and having roasted the long chine I pointed out to mortals the way into an abstruse art; and I brought to light the fiery symbols 42 that were aforetime wrapt in darkness. Such indeed were these boons; and the gains to mankind that were hidden under ground, brass, iron, silver, and gold—who could assert that he had discovered before me? No one, I well know, who does not mean to idly babble. And in one brief sentence learn the whole at once—All arts among the human race are from Prometheus.

Ch. Do not now serve the human race beyond what is profitable, nor disregard thyself in thy distress: since I have good hopes that thou shalt yet be liberated from these shackles, and be not one whit less powerful than Jove.

Pr. Not at all in this way is Fate, that brings events to their consummation ordained to accomplish these things: but 32 after having been bent by countless sufferings and calamities, thus am I to escape from my shackles. And art is far less powerful than necessity.

Ch. Who then is the pilot of necessity?

Pr. The triform Fates and the remembering Furies.

Ch. Is Jupiter then less powerful than these?

Pr. Most certainly he can not at any rate escape his doom. 43

Ch. Why, what is doomed for Jupiter but to reign for evermore?

Pr. This thou mayest not yet learn, and do not press it.

Ch. 'Tis surely some solemn mystery that thou veilest.

Pr. Make mention of some other matter; it is by no means seasonable to proclaim this; but it must be shrouded in deepest concealment; for it is by keeping this secret that I am to escape from my ignominious shackles and miseries.

Ch. Never may Jupiter, who directs all things, set his might in opposition to my purpose: nor may I be backward in attending upon the gods at their hallowed banquets, at which oxen are sacrificed, beside the restless stream of my sire Ocean; and may I not trespass in my words; but may this feeling abide by me and never melt away. Sweet it is to pass through a long life in confident hopes, making the spirits swell with bright merriment; but I shudder as I behold thee harrowed by agonies incalculable. For not standing in awe of Jupiter, thou, Prometheus, in thy self-will honorest mortals to excess. Come, my friend, own how boonless was the boon; say where is any aid? What relief can come from the creatures of a day? Sawest thou not the powerless weakness, nought better than a dream, in which 33 the blind race of men is entangled? Never shall at any time the schemes of mortals evade the harmonious system of Jupiter. This I learned by witnessing thy destructive fate, Prometheus. And far different is this strain that now flits toward me from the hymenæal chant which I raised around the baths and thy couch with the consent 44 of nuptials, when, after having won Hesione with thy love-tokens, thou didst conduct her our sister to be thy bride, the sharer of thy bed.

Enter Io . 45

What land is this? what race? whom shall I say I here behold storm-tossed in rocky fetters? Of what trespass is the retribution destroying thee? Declare to me into what part of earth I forlorn have roamed. Ah me! alas! alas! again the hornet 46 stings me miserable: O earth avert 47 the 34 goblin of earth-born Argus: 48 I am terrified at the sight of the neatherd of thousand eyes, for he is journeying on, keeping a cunning glance, whom not even after death does earth conceal; but issuing forth from among the departed he chases me miserable, and he makes me to wander famished along the shingled strand, while the sounding wax-compacted pipe drones on a sleepy strain. Oh! oh! ye powers! Oh! powers! whither do my far-roaming wanderings convey me? In what, in what, O son of Saturn, hast thou, having found me transgressing, shackled me in these pangs? Ah! ah! and art thus wearing out a timorous wretch frenzied with sting-driven fear. Burn me with fire, or bury me in earth, or give me for food to the monsters of the deep, and grudge me not these prayers, O king! Amply have my much-traversed wanderings harassed me; nor can I discover how I may avoid pain. Hearest thou the address of the ox-horned maiden?

Pr. How can I fail to hear the damsel that is frenzy-driven by the hornet, the daughter of Inachus, who warms 35 the heart of Jupiter with love, and now, abhorred of Juno, is driven perforce courses of exceeding length?

Io. From whence utterest thou the name of my father? Tell me, the woebegone, who thou art, who, I say, O hapless one, that hast thus correctly accosted me miserable, and hast named the heaven-inflicted disorder which wastes me, fretting with its maddening stings? Ah! ah! violently driven by the famishing tortures of my boundings have I come a victim to the wrathful counsels of Juno. And of the ill-fated who are there, ah me! that endure woes such as mine? But do thou clearly define to me what remains for me to suffer, what salve: 49 what remedy there is for my malady, discover to me, if at all thou knowest: speak, tell it to the wretched roaming damsel.

Pr. I will tell thee clearly every thing which thou desirest to learn, not interweaving riddles, but in plain language, as it is right to open the mouth to friends. Thou seest him that bestowed fire on mortals, Prometheus.

Io. O thou that didst dawn a common benefit upon mortals, wretched Prometheus, as penance for what offense art thou thus suffering?

Pr. I have just ceased lamenting my own pangs.

Io. Wilt thou not then accord to me this boon?

Pr. Say what it is that thou art asking, for thou mightest learn everything from me.

Io. Say who it was that bound thee fast in this cleft?

Pr. The decree of Jupiter, but the hand of Vulcan.

Io. And for what offenses art thou paying the penalty?

Pr. Thus much alone is all that I can clearly explain to thee.

36 Io. At least, in addition to this, discover what time shall be to me woe-worn the limit of my wanderings.

Pr. Not to learn this is better for thee than to learn it.

Io. Yet conceal not from me what I am to endure.

Pr. Nay, I grudge thee not this gift.

Io. Why then delayest thou to utter the whole?

Pr. 'Tis not reluctance, but I am loth to shock thy feelings.

Io. Do not be more anxious on my account than is agreeable to me. 50

Pr. Since thou art eager, I must needs tell thee: attend thou.

Ch. Not yet, however; but grant me also a share of the pleasure. Let us first learn the malady of this maiden, from her own tale of her destructive 51 fortunes; but, for the sequel of her afflictions let her be informed by thee.

Pr. It is thy part, Io, to minister to the gratification of these now before thee, both for all other reasons, and that they are the sisters of thy father. Since to weep and lament over misfortunes, when one is sure to win a tear from the listeners, is well worth the while.

Io. I know not how I should disobey you; and in a plain tale ye shall learn everything that ye desire; and yet I am pained even to speak of the tempest that hath been sent upon me from heaven, and the utter marring of my person, whence it suddenly came upon me, a wretched creature! For nightly visions thronging to my maiden chamber, would entice me 37 with smooth words: "O damsel, greatly fortunate, why dost thou live long time in maidenhood, when it is in thy power to achieve a match the very noblest? for Jupiter is fired by thy charms with the shaft of passion, and longs with thee to share in love. But do not, my child, spurn away from thee the couch of Jupiter; but go forth to Lerna's fertile mead, to the folds and ox-stalls of thy father, that the eye of Jove may have respite from its longing." By dreams such as these was I unhappy beset every night, until at length I made bold to tell my sire of the dreams that haunted me by night. And he dispatched both to Pytho and Dodona 52 many a messenger to consult the oracles, that he might learn what it behooved him to do or say, so as to perform what was well-pleasing to the divinities. And they came bringing a report back of oracles ambiguously worded, indistinct, and obscurely delivered. But at last a clear response came to Inachus, plainly charging and directing him to thrust me forth both from my home and my country, to stray an outcast to earth's remotest limits; and that, if he would not, a fiery-visaged thunderbolt would come from Jupiter, and utterly blot out his whole race. Overcome by oracles of Loxias such as these, unwilling did me expel and exclude me unwilling from his dwelling: but the bit of Jupiter 53 perforce constrained him to do this. And straightway my person and my mind were distorted, and horned, as ye see, stung by the keenly-biting fly, I rushed with maniac boundings to the sweet stream of Cerchneia, and the fountain 54 of Lerna; and the earth-born neatherd Argus of un 38 tempered fierceness, kept dogging me, peering after my footsteps with thickset eyes. Him, however, an unlooked-for sudden fate bereaved of life; but I hornet-stricken am driven by the scourge divine from land to land. Thou hearest what has taken place, and if thou art able to say what pangs there remain for me, declare them; and do not, compassionating me, warm me with false tales, for I pronounce fabricated statements to be a most foul malady.

Ch. Ah! ah! forbear! Alas! Never, never did I expect that a tale [so] strange would come to my ears, or that sufferings thus horrible to witness and horrible to endure, outrages, terrors with their two-edged goad, would chill my spirit. Alas! alas! O Fate! Fate! I shudder as I behold the condition of Io.

Pr. Prematurely, however, are thou sighing, and art full of terror. Hold, until thou shalt also have heard the residue.

Ch. Say on; inform me fully: to the sick indeed it is sweet to get a clear knowledge beforehand of the sequel of their sorrows.

Pr. Your former desire at any rate ye gained from me easily; for first of all ye desired to be informed by her recital of the affliction 55 that attaches to herself. Now give ear to the rest, what sort of sufferings it is the fate of this young damsel before you to undergo at the hand of Juno: thou too, seed of Inachus, lay to heart my words, that thou mayest be fully informed of the termination of thy journey. In the 39 first place, after turning thyself from this spot toward the rising of the sun, traverse unplowed fields; and thou wilt reach the wandering Scythians, who, raised from off the around, inhabit wicker dwellings on well-wheeled cars, equipped with distant-shooting bows; to whom thou must not draw near, but pass on out of their land, bringing thy feet to approach the rugged roaring shores. And on thy left hand dwell the Chalybes, workers of iron, of whom thou must needs beware, for they are barbarous, and not accessible to strangers. And thou wilt come to the river Hybristes, 56 not falsely so called, which do not thou cross, for it is not easy to ford, until thou shalt have come to Caucasus itself, loftiest of mountains, where from its very brow the river spouts forth its might. And surmounting its peaks that neighbor on the stars, thou must go into a southward track, where thou wilt come to the man-detesting host of Amazons, who hereafter shall make a settlement, Themiscyra, on the banks of Thermodon, where lies the rugged Salmydessian sea-gorge, a host by mariners hated, a step-dame to ships; and they will conduct thee on thy way, and that right willingly. Thou shalt come too to the Cimmerian isthmus, hard by the very portals of a lake, with narrow passage, which thou undauntedly must leave, and cross the Mæotic frith; and there shall exist for evermore among mortals a famous legend concerning thy passage, and after thy name it shall be called the Bosphorus; and after having quitted European ground, thou shalt come to the Asiatic continent. Does not then the sovereign of the gods seem to you to be violent alike toward all things? for he a god lusting to enjoy the charms of 40 this mortal fair one, hath cast upon her these wanderings. And a bitter wooer, maiden, hast thou found for thy hand; for think that the words which thou hast now heard are not even for a prelude.

Io. Woe is me! ah! ah!

Pr. Thou too in thy turn 57 art crying out and moaning: what wilt thou do then, when thou learnest the residue of thy ills?

Ch. What! hast thou aught of suffering left to tell to her?

Pr. Ay, a tempestuous sea of baleful calamities.

Io. What gain then is it for me to live? but why did I not quickly fling myself from this rough precipice, that dashing on the plain I had rid myself of all my pangs? for better is it once to die, than all one's days to suffer ill.

Pr. Verily thou wouldst hardly bear the agonies of me to whom it is not doomed to die. For this would be an escape from sufferings. But now there is no limit set to my hardships, until Jove shall have been deposed from his tyranny.

Io. What! is it possible that Jupiter should ever fall from his power?

Pr. Glad wouldst thou be, I ween, to witness this event.

Io. And how not so, I, who through Jupiter am suffering ill?

Pr. Well, then, thou mayest assure thyself of these things that they are so.

Io. By whom is he to be despoiled of his sceptre of tyranny.

Pr. Himself, by his own senseless counsels.

Io. In what manner? Specify it, if there be no harm.

Pr. He will make such a match as he shall one day rue. 58

41

Io. Celestial or mortal? If it may be spoken, tell me.

Pr. But why ask its nature? for it is not a matter that I can communicate to you.

Io. Is it by a consort that he is to be ejected from his throne?

Pr. Yes, surely, one that shall give birth to a son mightier than the father. 59

Io. And has he no refuge from this misfortune?

Pr. Not he, indeed, before at any rate I after being liberated from my shackles—

Io. Who, then, is he that shall liberate thee in despite of Jupiter?

Pr. It is ordained that it shall be one of thine own descendants.

Io. How sayest thou? Shall child of mine release thee from thy ills?

Pr. Yes, the third of thy lineage in addition to ten other generations. 60

42

Io. This prophecy of thine is no longer easy for me to form a guess upon.

Pr. Nor seek thou to know over well thine own pangs.

Io. Do not, after proffering me a benefit, withhold it from me.

Pr. I will freely grant thee one of two disclosures.

Io. Explain to me first of what sort they are, and allow me my choice.

Pr. I allow it thee; for choose whether I shall clearly tell to thee the residue of thy troubles, or who it is that is to be my deliverer.

Ch. Of these twain do thou vouchsafe to bestow the one boon on this damsel, and the other on me, and disdain thou not my request. To her tell the rest of her wanderings, and to me him that is to deliver thee; for this I long [to hear].

Pr. Seeing that ye are eagerly bent upon it, I will not oppose your wishes, so as not to utter every thing as much as ye desire. To thee in the first place, Io, will I describe thy mazy wanderings, which do thou engrave on the recording tablets of thy mind.

When thou shalt have crossed the stream that is the boundary of the Continents, to the ruddy realms of morn where walks the sun 61 . having passed over the roaring swell of the sea, until thou shalt reach the Gorgonian plains of Cisthene, where dwell the Phorcides, three swan-like aged damsels, that possess one eye in common, that have but a single tooth, on whom ne'er doth the sun glance with his rays, nor the nightly moon. And hard 43 by are three winged sisters of these, the snake-tressed Gorgons, abhorred of mortals, whom none of human race can look upon and retain the breath of life. 62 Such is this caution 63 which I mention to thee. Now lend an ear to another hideous spectacle; for be on thy guard against the keen-fanged hounds of Jupiter that never bark, the gryphons, and the cavalry host of one-eyed Arimaspians, who dwell on the banks of the gold-gushing fount, the stream of Pluto: go not thou nigh to these. And thou wilt reach a far-distant land, a dark tribe, who dwell close upon the fountains of the sun, where is the river Æthiops. Along the banks of this wend thy way, until thou shalt have reached the cataract where from the Bybline mountains the Nile pours forth his hallowed, grateful stream. This will guide thee to the triangular land of the Nile; where at length, Io, it is ordained for thee and thy children after thee to found the distant colony. And if aught of this is obscurely uttered, and hard to be understood, question me anew, and learn it thoroughly and clearly: as for leisure, I have more than I desire.

Ch. If indeed thou hast aught to tell of her baleful wanderings, that still remains or hath been omitted, say on; but if thou hast told the whole, give to us in our turn the favor which we ask, and you, perchance, remember.

Pr. She hath heard the full term of her journeying. And that she may know that she hath not been listening to me in vain, I will relate what hardships she endured before she came hither, giving her this as a sure proof of my state 44 ments. The very great multitude indeed of words I shall omit, and I will proceed to the termination itself of thine aberrations. For after that thou hadst come to the Molossian plains, and about the lofty ridge of Dodona, where is the oracular seat of Thesprotian Jove, and a portent passing belief, the speaking oaks, by which thou wast clearly and without any ambiguity saluted illustrious spouse of Jove that art to be; if aught of this hath any charms for thee. 64 Thence madly rushing along the seaside track, thou didst dart away to the vast bay of Rhea, from which thou art tempest-driven in retrograde courses: and in time to come, know well that the gulf of the deep shall be called IOnian, a memorial of thy passage to all mortals. These hast thou as tokens of my intelligence, how that it perceives somewhat beyond what appears.

The rest I shall tell both to you and to her in common, after reaching the very identical track of my former narrative. There is on the land's utmost verge a city Canopus, hard by the Nile's very mouth and alluvial dike; on this spot Jupiter at length makes thee sane by merely soothing and touching thee with his unalarming hand. And named after the progenitor of Jupiter 65 thou shalt give birth to swarthy Epaphus, who shall reap the harvest of all the land which the wide-streaming Nile waters. But fifth in descent 45 from him a generation of fifty virgins shall again come to Argos, not of their own accord, fleeing from incestuous wedlock with their cousins; and these with fluttering hearts, like falcons left not far behind by doves, shall come pursuing marriage such as should not be pursued, but heaven shall be jealous over their persons; 66 and Pelasgia shall receive them after being crushed by a deed of night-fenced daring, wrought by woman's hand; for each bride shall bereave her respective husband of life, having dyed in their throats 67 a sword of twin sharp edge. Would that in guise like this Venus might visit my foes! But tenderness shall soften one 68 of the maidens, so that she shall not slay the partner of her couch, but shall be blunt in her resolve; and of the two alternatives she shall choose the former, to be called a coward rather than a murderess. She in Argos shall give birth to a race of kings. There needs a long discourse to detail these things distinctly; but from this seed be sure shall spring a dauntless warrior renowned in archery, who shall set me free from these toils. Such predictions did my aged mother 46 the Titaness Themis rehearse to me; but how and when—to tell this requires a long detail, and thou in knowing it all wouldst be in nought a gainer.

Io. Eleleu! Eleleu! Once more the spasm 69 and maddening frenzies inflame me—and the sting of the hornet, wrought by no fire, 70 envenoms me; and with panic my heart throbs violently against my breast. My eyes, too, are rolling in a mazy whirl, and I am carried out of my course by the raging blast of madness, having no control of tongue, but my troubled words dash idly against the surges of loathsome calamity.

[*Exit* Io.

Ch. Wise was the man, ay, wise indeed, who first weighed well this maxim, and with his tongue published it abroad, that to match in one's own degree is best by far; 71 and that one who lives by labor should woo the hand neither of any that have waxed wanton in opulence, nor of such as pride themselves on nobility of birth. Never, O Destines, 72 never . may ye behold me approaching as a partner the couch of Jupiter: nor may I be 73 brought to the arms of any bridegroom from among the sons of heaven: for I am in dread when I behold the maiden Io, contented with no mortal lover, greatly marred by wearisome wanderings at the hand of Juno. For myself, indeed—inasmuch as wedlock on one's own level is free from apprehension—I feel no alarm. 74 And oh! never may the love of the mightier 47 gods cast on me a glance that none can elude. This at least is a war without a conflict, accomplishing things impossible: 75 nor know I what might become of me, for I see not how I could evade the counsel of Jove.

Pr. Yet truly shall Jove, albeit he is self-willed in his temper, be lowly, in such 76 wedlock is he prepared to wed, as shall hurl him out of his sovereignty and off his throne a forgotten thing; and the curse of his father Saturn shall then at length find entire consummation, which he imprecated when he was deposed from his ancient throne. From disasters such as these there is no one of the gods besides myself that can clearly disclose to him a way of escape. I know this, and by what means. Wherefore let him rest on in his presumption, putting confidence in his thunders aloft, brandishing in his hand a fire-breathing bolt. For not one jot shall these suffice to save him from falling dishonored in a downfall beyond endurance; such an antagonist is he now with his own hands preparing against himself, a portent that shall baffle all resistance; who shall invent a flame more potent than the lightning, and a mighty din that shall surpass the thunder; and shall shiver the ocean trident, that earth-convulsing pest, the spear of Neptune. And when he hath stumbled upon this mischief, he shall be taught how great is the difference between sovereignty and slavery.

Ch. Thou forsooth art boding against Jupiter the things thou wishest.

Pr. Things that shall come to pass, and that I desire to boot.

48

Ch. And are we to expect that any one will get the mastery of Jove?

Pr. Ay, and pangs too yet harder to bear than these [of mine] shall he sustain.

Ch. And how is it that thou art not dismayed blurting out words such as these?

Pr. Why at what should I be terrified to whom it is not destined to die?

Ch. Yet perchance he will provide for thee affliction more grievous than even this.

Pr. Let him do it then, all is foreseen by me.

Ch. They that do homage to Adrasteia are wise.

Pr. Do homage, make thy prayer, cringe to each ruler of the day. I care for Jove less than nothing; let him do, let him lord it for this brief span, e'en as he list, for not long shall he rule over the gods. But no more, for I descry Jove's courier close at hand, the menial of the new monarch: beyond all [doubt] he has come to announce to us some news.

Enter Mercury .

Thee, the contriver, thee full of gall and bitterness, who sinned against the gods by bestowing their honors on creatures of a day, the thief of fire, I address. The Sire commands thee to divulge of what nuptials it is that thou art vaunting, by means of which he is to be put down from his power. And these things, moreover, without any kind of mystery, but each exactly as it is, do thou tell out; and entail not upon me, Prometheus, a double journey; and thou perceivest that by such conduct Jove is not softened.

Pr. High sounding, i'faith, and full of haughtiness is thy speech, as beseems a lackey of the gods. Young in years, ye are young in power; 77 and ye fancy forsooth that ye dwell in 49 a citadel impregnable against sorrow. Have I not known two monarchs 78 dethroned from it? And the third that now is ruler I shall also see expelled most foully and most quickly. Seem I to thee in aught to be dismayed at, and to crouch beneath the new gods? Widely, ay altogether, do I come short [of such feelings]. But do thou hie thee back the way by which thou camest: for not one tittle shalt thou learn of the matter on which thou questionest me.

Mer. Yet truly 'twas by such self-will even before now that thou didst bring thyself to such a calamitous mooring.

Pr. Be well assured that I would not barter my wretched plight for thy drudgery; for better do I deem it to be a lackey to this rock, than to be born the confidential courier of father Jove. Thus is it meet to repay insult in kind.

Mer. Thou seemest to revel in thy present state.

Pr. Revel! Would that I might see my foes thus reveling, and among these I reckon thee.

Mer. What dost thou impute to me also any blame for thy mischances?

Pr. In plain truth, I detest all the gods, as many of them as, after having received benefits at my hands, are iniquitously visiting me with evils.

Mer. I hear thee raving with no slight disorder.

50

Pr. Disordered I would be, if disorder it be to loathe one's foes.

Mer. Thou wouldst be beyond endurance, wert thou in prosperity.

Pr. Woe's me!

Mer. This word of thine Jove knows not.

Pr. Ay, but Time as he grows old teaches all things.

Mer. And yet verily thou knowest not yet how to be discreet.

Pr. No i'faith, or I should not have held parley with thee, menial as thou art.

Mer. Thou seemest disposed to tell nought of the things which the Sire desires.

Pr. In sooth, being under obligation as I am to him, I am bound to return his favor.

Mer. Thou floutest me, forsooth, as if I were a boy.

Pr. Why, art thou not a boy, and yet sillier than one, if thou lookest to obtain any information from me? There is no outrage nor artifice by which Jupiter shall bring me to utter this, before my torturing shackles shall have been loosened. Wherefore let his glowing lightning be hurled, and with the white feathered shower of snow, and thunderings beneath the earth let him confound and embroil the universe; for nought of these things shall bend me so much as even to say by whom it is doomed that he shall be put down from his sovereignty.

Mer. Consider now whether this determination seems availing.

Pr. Long since has this been considered and resolved.

Mer. Resolve, O vain one, resolve at

length in consideration of thy present sufferings to come to thy right senses.

Pr. Thou troublest me with thine admonitions as vainly as 51 [thou mightest] a billow. 79 Never let it enter your thoughts that I, affrighted by the purpose of Jupiter, shall become womanish, and shall importune the object whom I greatly loathe, with effeminate upliftings of my hands, to release me from these shackles: I want much of that.

Mer. With all that I have said I seem to be speaking to no purpose; for not one whit art thou melted or softened in thy heart by entreaties, but art champing the bit like a colt fresh yoked, and struggling against the reins. But on the strength of an impotent scheme art thou thus violent; for obstinacy in one not soundly wise, itself by itself availeth less than nothing. And mark, if thou art not persuaded by my words, what a tempest and three-fold surge of ills, from which there is no escape, will come upon thee. For in the first place the Sire will shiver this craggy cleft with thunder and the blaze of his bolt, and will overwhelm thy body, and a clasping arm of rock shall bear thee up. And after thou shalt have passed through to its close, a long space of time, thou shalt come back into the light; and a winged hound of Jupiter, a blood-thirsty eagle, shall ravenously mangle thy huge lacerated frame, stealing upon thee an unbidden guest, and [tarrying] all the live-long day, and shall banquet his fill on the black viands 80 of thy liver. To such 52 labors look thou for no termination, until some god shall appear as a substitute in thy pangs, and shall be willing to go both to gloomy Hades, and to the murky depths around Tartarus. Wherefore advise thee, since this is no fictitious vaunt, but uttered in great earnestness; for the divine mouth knows not how to utter falsehood, but will bring every word to pass. But do thou look around and reflect, and never for a moment deem pertinacity better than discretion.

Ch. To us, indeed, Mercury seems to propose no unseasonable counsel; for he bids thee to abandon thy recklessness, and seek out wise consideration. Be persuaded; for to a wise man 'tis disgraceful to err.

Pr. To me already well aware of it hath this fellow urged his message; but for a foe to suffer horribly at the hands of foes is no indignity. Wherefore let the doubly-pointed wreath of his fire be hurled at me, and ether be torn piecemeal by thunder, and spasm of savage blasts; and let the wind rock earth from her base, roots and all, and with stormy surge mingle in rough tide the billow of the deep and the paths of the stars; and fling my body into black Tartarus, with a whirl, in the stern eddies of necessity. Yet by no possible means shall he visit me with death.

Mer. Resolutions and expressions, in truth, such as these of thine, one may hear from maniacs. For in what point doth his fate fall short of insanity? 81 What doth it abate from ravings? But do ye then at any rate, that sympathize with him in his sufferings, withdraw hence speedily some-whither from this spot, lest the harsh bellowing of the thunder smite you with idiotcy.

Ch. Utter and advise me to something else, in which too thou mayest prevail upon me; for in this, be sure, thou 53 hast intruded a proposal not to be borne. How is it that thou urgest me to practice baseness? Along with him here I am willing to endure what is destined, for I have learned to abhor traitors; and there is no evil which I hold in greater abomination.

Mer. Well, then, bear in mind the things of which I forewarn you: and do not, when ye have been caught in the snares of Atè, throw the blame on fortune, nor ever at any time say that Jove cast you into unforeseen calamity: no indeed, but ye your ownselves: for well aware, and not on a sudden, nor in ignorance, will ye be entangled by your senselessness in an impervious net of Atè.

[*Exit* Mercury .

Pr. And verily in deed and no longer in word doth the earth heave, and the roaring echo of thunder rolls bellowing by us; and deep blazing wreaths of lightning are glaring, and hurricanes whirl the dust; and blasts of all the winds are leaping forth, showing one against the other a strife of conflict gusts; and the firmament is embroiled with the deep. 82 Such is this onslaught that is clearly coming upon me from Jove, a cause for terror. O dread majesty of my mother Earth, O ether that diffusest thy common light, thou beholdest the wrongs I suffer.
54

THE SEVEN AGAINST THEBES.

The siege of the city of Thebes, and the description of the seven champions of the Theban and Argive armies, The deaths of the brothers Polynices and Eteocles, the mournings over them, by their sisters Antigone and Ismene, and the public refusal of burial to the ashes of Polynices, against which Antigone boldly protests, conclude the play.

PERSONS REPRESENTED.

Eteocles.	Ismene.
A Messenger.	Antigone.
Chorus of Theban Virgins.	A Herald.

Scene. The Acropolis of Thebes.—Compare v. 227, ed. Blomf.

Time. Early in the morning; the length of the action can scarcely be fixed with absolute certainty. It certainly did not exceed twelve hours.

The expedition of "the Seven" against Thebes is fixed by Sir I. Newton, B.C. 928. Cf. of his Chronology, p. 27. Blair carries it as far back as B.C. 1225.—Old Translator.

Eteocles. Citizens of Cadmus! it is fitting that he should speak things seasonable who has the care of affairs on the poop of a state, managing the helm, not lulling his eyelids in slumber. For if we succeed, the gods are the cause; but if, on the other hand (which heaven forbid), mischance should befall, Eteocles alone would be much bruited through the city by the townsmen in strains clamorous and in wailings, of which may Jove prove rightly called the Averter to 55 the city of the Cadmæans. 83 And now it behooves you—both him who still falls short of youth in its prime, and him who in point of age has passed his youth, nurturing the ample vigor of his frame and each that is in his prime, 84 as is best fitting—to succor the city, and the altars of your country's gods, so that their honors may never be obliterated; your children too, and your motherland, most beloved nurse; for she, taking fully on herself the whole trouble of your rearing, nurtured you when infants crawling on her kindly soil, for her trusty shield-bearing citizens, that ye might be [trusty 85] for this service. And, for the present indeed, up to this day, the deity inclines in our favor; since to us now all this time beleaguered the war for the most part, by divine allotment, turns out well. But now, as saith the seer, the feeder 86 of birds, revolving in ear and thoughts, without the use of fire, the oracular birds with unerring art—he, lord of such divining powers, declares that the main Achæan assault is this night proclaimed, 87 and [that the Achæans] attempt the city.

But haste ye all, both to the battlements and the gates of the tower works; On! in full panoply throng the breastworks, and take your stations on the platforms of the towers, and, making stand at the outlets of the gates, be of good 56 heart, nor be over-dismayed at the rabble of the aliens; God will give a happy issue. Moreover, I have also dispatched scouts and observers of the army, who will not, I feel assured, loiter on their way; and when I have had intelligence from these, I shall, in no point, be surprised by stratagem.

Messenger. —Most gallant Eteocles! sovereign of the Cadmæans, I have come bearing a clear account of the matters yonder, from the army; and I myself am eye-witness of the facts. For seven chieftains, impetuous leaders of battalions, cutting a bull's throat, 88 over an iron-rimmed shield, 89 and touching with their hands the gore of the bull, by oath have called to witness 90 Mars, Enyo, and Terror, that delights in bloodshed, that either having wrought the demolition of our city they will make havoc of the town of the Cadmæans, or having fallen will steep this land of ours in gore. Memorials too of themselves, to their parents at home, were they with their hands hanging in festoons 91 at the car of Adrastus, dropping a tear, but no sound of complaint passed their lips. 92 For their iron-hearted spirit glowing with valor was panting, as of lions that glare battle. And the report of these my tidings is not retarded by sluggishness. But I left them in the very act of casting lots, that so each of them, obtaining his post by lot, might lead on his battalion to our gates. Wherefore do thou with all speed marshal at the outlets of the gates the bravest men, the chosen of our city; for already the host of Argives hard at hand armed cap-à-pié 57 is in motion, is speeding onward, and white foam is staining the plain with its drippings from the lungs of their chargers. Do thou then, like the clever helmsman of a vessel, fence 93 our city before the breath of Mars burst like a hurricane upon it, for the main-land billow of their host is roaring. And for these measures do thou seize the very earliest opportunity; for the sequel I will keep my eye a faithful watch by day, and thou, knowing from the clearness of my detail the movements of those without, shalt be unscathed.

[*Exit* Messenger .

Et. O Jupiter! and earth! and ye tutelary deities! and thou Curse, the mighty Erinnys of my sire! do not, I pray, uproot with utter destruction from its very base, a prey to foemen, our city, which utters the language of Greece, and our native dwellings. 94 Grant that they may never hold the free land and city of Cadmus in a yoke of slavery; but be ye our strength—nay, I trust that I am urging our common interests, for a state that is in prosperity honors the divinities. 95

[*Exit* Eteocles .
58
Chorus. 96 I wail over our fearful, mighty woes! the army is let loose, having quitted its camp, a mighty mounted host is streaming hitherward in advance; 97 the dust appearing high in the air convinces me, a voiceless, clear, true messenger; the noise of the clatter of their hoofs upon the plain, 98 reaching even to our couches, approaches my ears, is wafted on, and is rumbling like a resistless torrent lashing the mountainside. Alas! alas! oh gods and goddesses, avert the rising horror; the white-bucklered 99 well-appointed host is rushing on with a shout on the other side our walls, speeding its way to the city. Who then will rescue us, who then of gods and goddesses will aid us? Shall I then prostrate myself before the statues of the divinities? Oh ye blessed beings, seated on your glorious thrones, 'tis high time for us to cling to your statues—why do we deeply sighing delay? Hear ye, or hear ye not, the clash of bucklers? When, if not now, 59 shall we set about the orison of the peplus 100 and chaplets? I perceive a din, a crash of no single spear. What wilt thou do? wilt thou, O Mars, ancient guardian of our soil, abandon thine own land? God of the golden helm, look upon, look upon the city which once thou didst hold well-beloved. Tutelary gods of our country, behold, 101 behold this train of virgins suppliant to escape from slavery, 102 for around our city a surge of men with waving crests is rippling, stirred by the blasts of Mars. But, O Jove, sire all-perfect! avert thoroughly from us capture by the foemen; for Argives are encircling the fortress of Cadmus; and I feel a dread of martial arms, and the bits which are fastened through the jaws of their horses are knelling slaughter. And seven leaders of the host, conspicuous in their spear-proof harness, are taking their stand at our seventh gate, 103 assigned their posts by lot. Do thou too, O Jove-born power that delightest in battle, Pallas, become a savior to our city; and thou, equestrian monarch, sovereign of the main, with thy fish-smiting trident, O Neptune, grant a deliverance, a deliverance from our terrors. Do thou too, O Mars, alas! alas! guard the city which is named after Cadmus, and manifestly show thy care 60 —and thou, Venus, the original mother of our race, avert [these ills]— for from thy blood are we sprung; calling on thee with heavenward orisons do we approach thee. And thou, Lycæan

king, be thou fierce as a wolf 104 to the hostile army, [moved] by the voice of our sighs. 105 Thou too, virgin-daughter of Latona, deftly adorn thyself with thy bow, O beloved Diana. Ah! ah! ah! I hear the rumbling of cars around the city, O revered Juno, the naves of the heavy-laden axles creak, the air is maddened with the whizzing of javelins—what is our city undergoing? What will become of it? To what point is the deity conducting the issue? 106 ah! ah! A shower of stones too from their slingers is coming over our battlements. O beloved Apollo! there is the clash of brass-rimmed shields at the gates, and the just issue in battle must be decided by arms according to the disposal of Jove. 107 And thou Onca, 108 immortal queen, that dwellest in front of our city, rescue thy seven-gated seat. O gods, all-potent to save, O ye gods and goddesses, perfect guardians of the towers of this land, abandon not our war-wasted city to an army of aliens. Listen to these virgins, listen to our all-just prayers, as is most right, to the orisons of virgins which are offered with outstretched hands. O 61 beloved divinities, hovering around our city as its deliverers, show how ye love it; give heed to our public rituals, and when ye give heed to them succor us, and be ye truly mindful, I beseech ye, of the rites of our city which abound in sacrifices.

Re-enter Eteocles .

Intolerable creatures! is this, I ask you, best and salutary for our city, and an encouragement to this beleagured force, for you to fall before the statues of our tutelary gods, to shriek, to yell—O ye abominations of the wise. Neither in woes nor in welcome prosperity may I be associated with womankind; for when woman prevails, her audacity is more than one can live with; and when she is affrighted, she is a still greater mischief to her home and city. Even now, having brought upon your countrymen this pell-mell flight, ye have, by your outcries, spread dastard cowardice, and ye are serving, as best ye may, the interests of those without, but we within our walls are suffering capture at our own hands; such blessings will you have if you live along with women. Wherefore if any one give not ear to my authority, be it man or woman, or other between [these names 109], the fatal pebble shall decide against him, and by no means shall he escape the doom of stoning at the hand of the populace. For what passeth without is a man's concern, let not woman offer advice—but remaining within do thou occasion no mischief. Heard'st thou, or heard'st thou not, or am I speaking to a deaf woman?

Ch. O dear son of Œdipus, I felt terror when I heard the din from the clatter of the cars, when the wheel-whirling naves rattled, and [the din] of the fire-wrought bits, the rudders 110 of the horses, passing through their mouths that know no rest.

62

Et. What then? does the mariner who flees from the stern to the prow 111 find means of escape, when his bark is laboring against the billow of the ocean?

Ch. No; but I came in haste to the ancient statues of the divinities, trusting in the gods, when there was a pattering at our gates of destructive sleet showering down, even then I was carried away by terror to offer my supplications to the Immortals, that they would extend their protection over the city.

Et. Pray that our fortification may resist the hostile spear.

Ch. Shall not this, then, be at the disposal of the gods?

Et. Ay, but 'tis said that the gods of the captured city abandon it.

Ch. At no time during my life may this conclave of gods abandon us: never may I behold our city overrun, and an army firing it with hostile flame.

Et. Do not thou, invoking the gods, take ill counsel; for subordination, woman, is the mother of saving success; so the adage runs.

Ch. But the gods have a power superior still, and oft in adversity does this raise the helpless out of severe calamity, when clouds are overhanging his brow.

Et. It is the business of men, to present victims and offer 63 ings of worship to the gods, when foemen are making an attempt: 'tis thine on the other hand to hold thy peace and abide within doors.

Ch. 'Tis by the blessing of the gods that we inhabit a city unconquered, and that our fortification is proof against the multitude of our enemies. What Nemesis can feel offended at this?

Et. I am not offended that ye should honor the race of the gods; but that thou mayest not render the citizens faint-hearted, keep quiet and yield not to excessive terrors.

Ch. When I heard the sudden din, I came, on the very instant, in distracting panic to this Acropolis, a hallowed seat.

Et. Do not now, if ye hear of the dying or the wounded, eagerly receive them with shrieks; for with this slaughter of mortals is Mars fed.

Ch. And I do in truth hear the snortings of the horses.

Et. Do not now, when thou hearest them, hear too distinctly.

Ch. Our city groans from the ground, as though the foes were hemming her in.

Et. Is it not then enough that I take measures for this?

Ch. I fear! for the battering at the gates increases.

Et. Wilt thou not be silent? Say nought of this kind in the city.

Ch. O associate band [of gods], abandon not our towers.

Et. Can not ye endure it in silence, and confusion to ye?

Ch. Gods of my city! let me not meet with slavery.

Et. Thou thyself art making a slave both of me, of thyself, and of the city.

Ch. O all-potent Jove! turn the shaft against our foes.

Et. O Jove! what a race hast thou made women! 64

Ch. Just as wretched as men when their city is taken.

Et. Again thou art yelping as thou claspest the statues!

Ch. Yes, for in my panic terror hurries away my tongue.

Et. Would to heaven that you would grant me a trifling favor on my requesting it.

Ch. Tell me as quickly as you can,

and I shall know at once.

Et. Hold thy peace, wretched woman, alarm not thy friends.

Ch. I hold my peace—with others I will suffer what is destined.

Et. I prefer this expression of thine rather than thy former words; and moreover, coming forth from the statues, pray thou for the best—that the gods may be our allies. And after thou hast listened to my prayers, then do thou raise the sacred auspicious shout of the Pæan, the Grecian rite of sacrificial acclamation, an encouragement to thy friends that removes the fear of the foe. And I, to the tutelary gods of our land, both those who haunt the plains, and those who watch over the forum, and to the fountains of Dirce, and I speak not without those of the Ismenus, 112 if things turn out well and our city is preserved, do thus make my vows that we, dyeing the altars of the gods with the blood of sheep, offering bulls to the gods, will deposit trophies, and vestments of our enemies, spear-won spoils of the foe, in their hallowed abodes. Offer thou prayers like these to the gods, not with a number of sighs, nor with foolish and wild sobbings; for not one whit the more wilt thou escape 65 Destiny. But I too, forsooth, 113 will go and marshal at the seven outlets of our walls, six men, with myself for a seventh, antagonists to our foes in gallant plight, before both urgent messengers and quickly-bruited tidings arrive, and inflame us by the crisis.

[*Exit* Eteocles .

Ch. I attend, but through terror my heart sleeps not, and cares that press close upon my heart keep my dread alive, because of the host that hems our walls 114 around; like as a dove, an all-attentive nurse, fears, on behalf of her brood, serpents, evil intruders into her nest. For some are advancing against the towers in all their numbers, in all their array; (what will become of me?) and others are launching the vast rugged stone at the citizens, who are assailed on all sides. By every means, O ye Jove-descended gods! rescue the city and the army that spring from Cadmus. What better plain of land will ye take in exchange to yourselves than this, after ye have abandoned to our enemies the fertile land, and Dirce's water best fed of all the streams that earth-encircling Neptune sends forth, and the daughters of Tethys? Wherefore, O tutelary gods of the city! having hurled on those without the towers the calamity that slaughters men, and casts away shields, achieve glory for these citizens, and be your statues placed on noble sites, as deliverers of our city, 115 through our entreaties fraught with 66 shrill groanings. For sad it is to send prematurely to destruction an ancient city, a prey of slavery to the spear, ingloriously overthrown in crumbling ashes by an Achæan according to the will of heaven; and for its women to be dragged away captives, alas! alas! both the young and the aged, like horses by their hair, while their vestments are rent about their persons. And the emptied city cries aloud, while its booty is wasted amid confused clamors; verily I fearfully forbode heavy calamities. And a mournful thing it is for [maidens] just marriageable, 116 before the celebration of rites for culling the fresh flower of their virginity, to have to traverse a hateful journey from their homes. What? I pronounce that the dead fares better than these; for full many are the calamities, alas! alas! which a city undergoes when it has been reduced. One drags another, 117 slaughters, and to parts he sets fire—the whole city is defiled with smoke, and raving Mars that tramples down the nations, violating piety, inspires them. Throughout the town are uproars, against the city rises the turreted circumvallation, 118 and man is slain by man with the spear. And the cries of children at the breast all bloody resound, and there is rapine sister of pell-mell confusion. Pillager meets pillager, and the empty-handed shouts to the empty-handed, wishing to have a partner, greedy for a portion that shall be neither less nor equal. What of these things can speech picture? Fruits of every possible kind strewn 119 upon the ground occasion 67 sorrow, and dismal is the face of the stewards. And full many a gift of earth is swept along in the worthless streams, in undistinguished medley. And young female slaves have new sorrows, a foe being superior 120 and fortunate as to their wretched captive couch, so that they hope for life's gloomy close to come, a guardian against their all-mournful sorrows.

Semi-Ch. The scout, methinks, my friends, is bringing us some fresh tidings from the army, urging in haste the forwarding axles 121 of his feet.

Semi-Ch. Ay, and in very truth, here comes our prince, son of Œdipus, very opportunely for learning the messenger's report—and haste does not allow him to make equal footsteps. 122

[*Re-enter* Messenger *and* Eteocles *from different sides.*

Mes. I would fain tell, for I know them well, the arrangements of our adversaries, and how each has obtained his lot at our gate. Tydeus now for some time has been raging hard by the gates of Prœtus; but the seer allows him not to cross the stream of Ismenus, for the sacrifices are not auspicious. So Tydeus, raving and greedy for the fight, roars like a serpent in its hissings beneath the noontide heat, and he smites the sage seer, son of Oïcleus, with a taunt, [saying] that he 68 is crouching to both Death and Battle out of cowardice. Shouting out such words as these, he shakes there shadowy crests, the hairy honors of his helm, while beneath his buckler bells cast in brass are shrilly pealing terror: on his buckler too he has this arrogant device—a gleaming sky tricked out with stars, and in the centre of the shield a brilliant full moon is conspicuous, most august of the heavenly bodies, the eye of night. Chafing thus in his vaunting harness, he roars beside the bank of the river, enamored of conflict, like a steed champing his bit with rage, that rushes forth when he hears the voice of the trumpet. 123 Whom wilt thou marshal against this [foe]? Who, when the fastenings give way, is fit to be intrusted with the defense of the gate of Prœtus?

Et. At no possible array of a man should I tremble; and blazonry has no power of inflicting wounds, and crests and bell bite not 124 without the spear. And for this night which thou tellest me is sparkling on his buckler with the stars of heaven, it may perchance be a prophet in conceit; 125 for if night shall settle on his eyes as he is dying, verily this vaunting device would correctly and justly answer to its name, and he himself will have the insolence ominous 69 against himself. But against Tydeus will I marshal this wary son of Astacus, as defender of the portals, full nobly born, and one that reverences the throne of Modesty, and detests too haughty language, for he is wont to be slow at base acts, but no dastard. And from the sown heroes whom Mars spared is Melanippus sprung a scion, and he is thoroughly a native. But the event Mars with his dice will decide. And justice, his near kinswoman, makes him her champion, 126 that he may ward off the foeman's spear from the mother that bare him.

Ch. Now may the gods grant unto our champion to be successful, since with justice 127 does he speed forth in defense of the city; but I shudder to behold the sanguinary fate of those who perish in behalf of their friends.

Mes. To him may the gods so grant success. But Capaneus has by lot obtained his station against the Electran gate. This is a giant, greater than the other aforementioned, and his vaunt savors not of humanity; but he threatens horrors against our towers, which may fortune not bring to pass! for he declares, that whether the god is willing or unwilling, he will make havoc of our city, and that not the Wrath 128 of Jove, dashing down upon the plain, should stop him. And he is wont to compare both the lightnings and the thunder-bolts to the heat of noontide. He has a bearing 70 too, a naked man bearing fire, and there gleams a torch with which his hands are armed; 129 and, in letters of gold, he is uttering, I will burn the city. Against a man such as this do thou send 130 ——. Who will engage with him? Who will abide his vaunting and not tremble?

Et. And in this case 131 also one advantage is gained upon another. Of the vain conceits of man in sooth the tongue of truth becomes accuser. But Capaneus is menacing, prepared for action, dishonoring the gods, and practicing his tongue in vain exultation; mortal as he is, he is sending loud-swelling words into heaven to the ears of Jove. But I trust that, as he well deserves, the fire-bearing thunder-bolt will with justice come upon him, in no wise likened to the noontide warmth of the sun. Yet against him, albeit he is a very violent blusterer, is a hero marshaled, fiery in his spirit, stout Polyphontes, a trusty guard by the favor of Diana our protectress, and of the other gods. Mention another who hath had his station fixed at another of our gates.

Ch. May he perish 132 who proudly vaunts against our city, and may the thunder-bolt check him before that he bursts into my abode, or ever, with his insolent spear force us away from our maiden dwellings.

Mes. And verily I will mention him that hath next had 71 his post allotted against our gates: for to Eteoclus, third in order, hath the third lot leapt from the inverted helm of glittering brass, for him to advance his battalion against the gates of Neïs; and he is wheeling his steeds fuming in their trappings, eager to dash forward against the gates. And their snaffles ring, in barbarian fashion, filled with the breath of their snorting nostrils. His buckler, too, hath been blazoned in no paltry style, but a man in armor is treading the steps of a ladder to his foemen's tower, seeking to storm it. And this man, in a combination of letters, is shouting, how that not even Mars should force him from the bulwarks. Do thou send also to this man a worthy champion to ward off from this city the servile yoke.

Et. I will send this man forthwith, and may it be with good fortune; and verily he is sent, bearing his boast in deed, 133 Megareus, the offspring of Creon, of the race of the sown; 134 who will go forth from the gates not a whit terrified at the noise of the mad snortings of the horses; but, either by his fall will fully pay the debt of his nurture to the land, or, having taken two men 135 and the city on the shield, will garnish with the spoils the house of his father. Vaunt thee of another, and spare me not the recital.

Ch. I pray that this side may succeed, O champion of my dwellings! and that with them it may go ill; and as they, with frenzied mind, utter exceedingly proud vaunts against our city, so may Jove the avenger regard them in his wrath.

Mes. Another, the fourth, who occupies the adjoining gates of Onca Minerva, stands hard by with a shout, the 72 shape and mighty mould of Hippomedon; and I shuddered at him as he whirled the immense orb, I mean the circumference of his buckler—I will not deny it. And assuredly it was not any mean artificer in heraldry who produced this work upon his buckler, a Typhon, darting forth through his fire-breathing mouth dark smoke, the quivering sister of fire, and the circular cavity of the hollow-bellied shield hath been made farther solid with coils of serpents. He himself, too, hath raised the war-cry; and, possessed by Mars, raves for the onslaught, like a Thyiad, 136 glaring terror. Well must we guard against the attack of such a man as this, for Terror is already vaunting himself hard by our gates.

Et. In the first place, this Onca Pallas, who dwells in our suburbs, living near the gates, detesting the insolence of the man, will drive him off, as a noxious serpent from her young. And Hyperbius, worthy son of Œnops, hath been chosen to oppose him, man to man, willing to essay his destiny in the crisis of fortune; he is open to censure neither in form, nor in spirit, nor in array of arm: but Mercury hath matched them fairly; for hostile is the man to the man with whom he will have to combat, and on their bucklers will they bring into conflict hostile gods; for the one hath fire-breathing Typhon, and on the buckler of Hyperbius father Jove is seated firm, flashing, with his bolt in his hand; and never yet did any one know of Jove being by any chance vanquished. 137 Such in good sooth is the friend 73 ship of the divinities: we are on the side of the victors, but they on that of the conquered, if at least Jove be mightier in battle than Typhon. Wherefore 'tis probable that the combatants will fare accordingly; and to Hyperbius, in accordance with its blazonry, may Jove that is on his shield become a savior.

Ch. I feel confident that he who hath upon his shield the adversary of Jove, the hateful form of the subterranean fiend, a semblance hateful both to mortals and the everliving gods, will have to leave his head before our gates.

Mes. May such be the issue! But, farthermore, I mention the fifth, marshaled at the fifth gate, that of Boreas, by the very tomb of Jove-born Amphion. And he makes oath by the spear 138 which he grasps, daring to revere it more than a god, and more dearly than his eyes, 139 that verily he will make havoc of the city of the Cadmæans in spite of Jove: thus says the fair-faced scion of a mountain-dwelling mother, a stripling hero, and the down is just making its way through his cheeks, in the spring of his prime, thick sprouting hair. And he takes his post, having a ruthless spirit, not answering to his maidenly name, 140 and a savage aspect. Yet not 74 without his vaunt does he take stand against our gates, for on his brazen-forged shield the rounded bulwark of his body, he was wielding the reproach of our city, the Sphinx of ruthless maw affixed by means of studs, a gleaming embossed form; and under her she holds a man, one of the Cadmæans, so that against this man 141 most shafts are hurled. And he, a youth, Parthenopæus an Arcadian, seems to have come to fight in no short measure, 142 and not to disgrace the length of way that he has traversed; for this man, such as he is, is a sojourner, and, by way of fully repaying Argos for the goodly nurture she has given him, he utters against these towers menaces, which may the deity not fulfill.

Et. O may they receive from the gods the things which they are purposing in those very unhallowed vaunts! Assuredly they would perish most miserably in utter destruction. But there is [provided] for this man also, the Arcadian of whom you speak, a man that is no braggart, but his hand discerns what should be done, Actor, brother of the one aforementioned, who will not allow either a tongue, without deeds, streaming within our gates, to aggravate mischiefs, nor him to make his way within who bears upon his hostile buckler the image of the wild beast, most odious monster, which from the outside shall find fault with him who bears it within, when it meets with a thick battering under the city. So, please the gods, may I be speaking the truth.

Ch. The tale pierces my bosom, the locks of my hair stand erect, when I hear of the big words of these proudly 75 vaunting impious men. Oh! would that the gods would destroy them in the land.

Mes. I will tell of the sixth, a man most prudent, and in valor the best, the seer, the mighty Amphiaraus; for he, having been marshaled against the gate of Homolöis, reviles mighty Tydeus full oft with reproaches, as the homicide, the troubler of the state, chief teacher of the mischiefs of Argos, the summoner of Erinnys, minister of slaughter, and adviser of these mischiefs to Adrastus. Then again going up 143 to thy brother, the mighty Polynices, he casts his eye aloft, and, at last, reproachfully dividing his name [into syllables, 144] he calls to him: and through his mouth he gives utterance to this speech—"Verily such a deed is well-pleasing to the gods, and glorious to hear of and to tell in after times, that you are making havoc of your paternal city, and its native gods, having brought into it a foreign armament. And what Justice shall staunch the fountain of thy mother's tears?

76

And how can thy father-land, after having been taken by the spear through thy means, ever be an ally to thee? I, for my part, in very truth shall fatten this soil, seer as I am, buried beneath a hostile earth. Let us to the battle, I look not for a dishonorable fall." Thus spake the seer, wielding a fair-orbed shield, all of brass; but no device was on its circle—for he wishes not to seem but to be righteous, reaping fruit from a deep furrow in his mind, from which sprout forth his goodly counsels. Against this champion I advise that thou send antagonists, both wise and good. A dread adversary is he that reveres the gods.

Et. Alas! for the omen 145 that associates a righteous man with the impious! Indeed in every matter, nothing is worse than evil fellowship—the field of infatuation has death for its fruits. 146 For whether it be that a pious man hath embarked in a vessel along with violent sailors, and some villany, he perishes with the race of men abhorred of heaven; or, being righteous, and having rightly fallen into the same toils with his countrymen, violators of hospitality, and unmindful of the gods, he is beaten down, smitten with the scourge of the deity, which falls alike on all. Now this seer, I mean the son of Oïcleus, a moderate, just, good, and pious man, a mighty prophet, associated with unholy bold-mouthed men, in spite of his [better] judgment, when they made their long march, by the favor of Jove, shall be drawn along with them to go to the distant city. 147 I fancy, indeed, that he 77 will not make an attack on our gates, not as wanting spirit, nor from cowardice of disposition, but he knows that it is his doom to fall in battle, if there is to be any fruit in the oracles of Apollo: 'tis his wont too to hold his peace, or to speak what is seasonable. Nevertheless against him we will marshal a man, mighty Lasthenes, a porter surly to strangers, and who bears an aged mind, but a youthful form; quick is his eye, and he is not slow of hand to snatch his spear made naked from his left hand. 148 But for mortals to succeed is a boon of the deity.

Ch. O ye gods, give ear to our righteous supplications, and graciously bring it to pass that our city may be successful, while ye turn the horrors wrought by the spear upon the invaders of our country; and may Jove, having flung them [to a distance] from our towers, slay them with his thunder-bolt.

Mes. Now will I mention this the seventh, against the seventh gate, thine own brother—what calamities too he imprecates and prays for against our city; that, he having scaled the towers, and been proclaimed 149 to the land, after having shouted out the pæan of triumph at the capture, may engage with thee; and, having slain thee, may die beside thee, or avenge himself on thee alive, that dishonored, that banished him, 150 by exile after the very same manner. This does mighty Polynices clamor, and he summons the gods of his race and 78 fatherland to regard his supplications. He has, moreover, a newly-constructed shield, well suited [to his arm] and a double device wrought upon it. For a woman is leading on a mailed warrior, forged out of brass, conducting him decorously; and so she professes to be Justice, as the inscription tells: I will bring back this man, and he shall have the city of his fathers, and a dwelling in the palace . Such are their devices; and do thou thyself now determine whom it is that thou thinkest proper to send: since never at any time shalt thou censure me for my tidings; but do thou thyself determine the management of the vessel of the state.

Et. O heaven-frenzied, and great abomination of the gods! Oh! for our race of Œdipus, worthy of all mourning—Alas for me! now verily are the curses of my sire coming to an accomplishment. But it becomes me not to weep or wail, lest birth be given to a lament yet more intolerable. But to Polynices, that well deserves his name, I say, soon shall we know what issue his blazonry will have; whether letters wrought in gold, vainly vaunting on his buckler, along with frenzy of soul will restore him. If indeed Justice, the virgin daughter of Jove, attended on his actions or his thoughts, perchance this might be. But neither when he escape the darkness of the womb, nor in his infancy, nor ever in his boyhood, nor in the gathering of the hair on his chin, did Justice look on him, or deem him worthy her regards: nor truly do I suppose that she will now take her stand near to him, in his ill-omened possession of his father-land. Truly she would then in all reason be falsely called Justice, were she to consort with a man all-daring in his soul. Trusting in this I will go, and face him in person. Who else could do so with better right? Leader against leader, brother against brother, foeman with 79 foeman, shall I take my stand. Bring me with all speed my greaves, my spear, and my armor of defense against the stones.

[*Exit* Messenger .

Ch. Do not, O dearest of men, son of Œdipus, become in wrath like to him against whom thou hast most bitterly spoken. Enough it is that Cadmæans come to the encounter with Argives. For such bloodshed admits of expiation. But the death of own brothers thus mutually wrought by their own hands—of this pollution there is no decay.

Et. If any one receives evil without disgrace, be it so; for the only advantage is among the dead: but of evil and disgraceful things, thou canst not tell me honor.

Ch. Why art thou eager, my son? let not Atè, full of wrath, raging with the spear, hurry thee away—but banish the first impulse of [evil] passion.

Et. Since the deity with all power urges on the matter, let the whole race of Laius, abhorred by Phœbus, having received for its portion the wave of Cocytus, drift down with the wind.

Ch. So fierce a biting lust for unlawful blood hurries thee on to perpetrate the shedding of a man's blood, of which the fruit is bitter. 151

Et. Ay, for the hateful curse of my dear father, consummated, sits hard beside me with dry tearless eyes, telling me that profit comes before my after doom. 152

Ch. But do not accelerate it; thou wilt not be called dastardly if thou honorably preservest thy life—and Erinnys, 153 80 with her murky tempest, enters not the dwelling where the gods receive a sacrifice from the hands [of the inmates].

Et. By the gods, indeed, we have now for some time been in a manner neglected, and the pleasure which arises from our destruction is welcomed by them; why should we any longer fawn 154 upon our deadly doom?

Ch. Do so now, while it is in thy power; since the demon, that may alter with a distant shifting of his temper, will perchance come with a gentler air; but now he still rages.

Et. Ay, for the curses of Œdipus have raged beyond all bounds; and too true were my visions of phantoms seen in my slumbers, dividers of my father's wealth. 155

Ch. Yield thee to women, albeit that thou lovest them not.

Et. Say ye then what one may allow you; but it must not be at length.

Ch. Go not thou on in this way to the seventh gate.

Et. Whetted as I am, thou wilt not blunt me by argument.

Ch. Yet god, at all events, honors an inglorious victory.

Et. It ill becomes a warrior to acquiesce in this advice.

Ch. What! wilt thou shed the blood of thine own brother?

Et. By heaven's leave, he shall not elude destruction.

[*Exit* Eteocles .

Ch. I shudder with dread that the power that lays waste this house, not like the gods, the all-true, the evil-boding Erinnys summoned by the curses of the father, is bringing 81 to a consummation the wrathful curses of distracted Œdipus. 156 'Tis this quarrel, fatal to his sons, that arouses her. And the Chalybian stranger, emigrant from Scythia, is apportioning their shares, a fell divider of possessions, the stern-hearted steel, 157 allotting them land to occupy, just as much as it may be theirs to possess when dead, bereft of their large domains. 158 When they shall have fallen, slain by each other's hands in mutual slaughter, and the dust of the ground shall have drunk up the black-clotted blood of murder, who will furnish expiation? who will purify them? Alas for the fresh troubles mingled with the ancient horrors of this family! for I speak of the ancient transgression with its speedy punishment; yet it abides unto the third generation; since Laïus, in spite of Apollo, who had thrice declared, in the central oracles of Pytho, that, dying without issue, he would save the state, 159 did, notwithstanding, overcome by his friends, in his infatuation beget his own destruction, the parricide Œdipus, who dared to plant in an unhallowed 82 field, where he had been reared, a bloody root.—'Twas frenzy linked the distracted pair; and as it were, a sea of troubles brings on one billow that subsides, and rears another triply cloven, which too dashes about the stern of our state. But between [it and us] there stretches a fence at a small interval, a tower in width alone. 160 And I fear lest the city should be overcome along with its princes. For the execrations, that were uttered long ago, are finding their accomplishment: bitter is the settlement, and deadly things in their consummation pass not away. The wealth of enterprising merchants, 161 too thickly stowed, brings with it a casting overboard from the stern. For whom of mortals did the gods, and his fellow-inmates in the city, and the many lives of herding men, 162 admire so much as they then honored Œdipus, who had banished from the realm the baneful pest that made men her prey. But when he unhappy was apprised of his wretched marriage, despairing in his sorrow, with frenzied heart, he perpetrated a two-fold horror; he deprived himself with parricidal hand of the eyes that were more precious than his children. And indignant because of his scanty supply of food, 163 he sent upon his sons, alas! alas! a curse horrible in utterance, even that they should some time or other share his substance between them with sword-wielding hand; and now I tremble lest the swift Erinnys should be on the point of fulfilling that prayer.

83

Re-enter Messenger .

Be of good cheer, maidens that have been nurtured by your mothers. 164 This city hath escaped the yoke of servitude; the vauntings of our mighty foes have fallen; and our city is calm, and hath not admitted a leak from the many buffets of the surge; our fortification too stands proof, and we have fenced our gates with champions fighting single-handed, and bringing surety; for the most part, at six of our gates, it is well; but the seventh, the revered lord of the seventh, sovereign Apollo, chose for himself, bringing to a consummation the ancient indiscretions of Laïus.

Ch. And what new event is happening to our city?

Mes. These men have fallen by hands that dealt mutual slaughter. 165 —

Ch. Who? What is it thou sayest! I am distracted with terror at thy tidings.

Mes. Now be calm and listen, the race of Œdipus—

Ch. Alas for me wretched! I am a prophetess of horrors.

Mes. Stretched in the dust are they beyond all dispute.

Ch. Came they even to that? bitter then are thy tidings, yet speak them.

Mes. Even thus [too surely] were they destroyed by brotherly hands.

Ch. Even thus was the demon at once impartial to both.

84

Mes. And he himself, to be sure of this, is cutting off the ill-fated race.

Ch. Over such events one may both rejoice and weep—[rejoice] at the success of our city—but [mourn because] 166 our princes, the two generals, have portioned out the whole possession of their substance with the hammer-wrought Scythian steel, and they will possess of land just as much as they receive at their burial, carried off according to the unhappy imprecations of their sire.

Mes. The city is rescued, but earth hath drank the blood of the brother princes through their slaughter of each other.

[*Exit* Messenger . 167

Ch. Oh mighty Jove! and tutelary divinities of our city! ye that do in very deed protect these towers of Cadmus, am I to rejoice and raise a joyous hymn to the savior of our city, the averter of mischief, or shall I bewail the miserable and ill-fated childless 168 commanders, who, in very truth, correctly, according to their name, 169 full of rancor, have per 85 ished in impious purpose? Oh dark and fatal curse of the race and of Œdipus, what horrible chill is this that is falling upon my heart? 170 I, like a Thyiad, have framed a dirge for the tomb, hearing of the dead, dabbled in blood, that perished haplessly—verily this meeting of spears was ill-omened. The imprecation of the father hath taken full effect, and hath not failed: and the unbelieving schemes of Laïus have lasted even until now; and care is through our city, and the divine declarations lose not their edge—Alas! worthy of many a sigh, ye have accomplished this horror surpassing credence; and lamentable sufferings have come indeed. This is self-evident, the tale of the messenger is before my eyes—Double are our sorrows, double are the horrors of them that have fallen by mutual slaughter; doubly shared are these consummated sufferings. What shall I say? What, but that of a certainty troubles on troubles are constant inmates of this house? But, my friends, ply the speeding stroke of your hands about your heads, before the gale of sighs, which ever wafts on its passage the bark, on which no sighs are heard, with sable sails, the freighted with the dead, untrodden for Apollo, the sunless, across Acheron, and to the invisible all-receiving shore. 171

But [enough]! for here are coming to this bitter office both Antigone and Ismene. I am assured beyond all doubt that they will send forth a fitting wail from their lovely deep-cinctured bosoms. And right it is that we, before the 86 sound of their wailing reach us, both ejaculate the dismal-sounding chaunt of Erinnys, and sing a hateful pæan to Pluto. Alas! ye that are the most hapless in your sisterhood of all women that fling the zone around their robes, I weep, I mourn, and there is no guile about so as not to be truly wailing from my very soul.

Semi-Chorus. Alas! alas! ye frantic youths, distrustful of friends, and unsubdued by troubles, have wretched seized on your paternal dwelling with the spear.

Semi-Ch. Wretched in sooth were they who found a wretched death to the bane of their houses.

Semi-Ch. Alas! alas! ye that overthrew the walls of your palace, and having cast an eye on bitter monarchy, how have ye now settled your claims with the steel?

Semi-Ch. And too truly hath awful Erinnys brought [the curses] of their father Œdipus to a consummation.

Semi-Ch. Smitten through your left—Smitten in very truth, and through sides that sprung from a common womb.

Semi-Ch. Alas for them, wretched! Alas! for the imprecations of death which avenged murder by murder.

Semi-Ch. Thou speakest of the stroke that pierced through and through those that were smitten in their houses and in their persons with speechless rage, and the doom of discord brought upon them by the curses of their father.

Semi-Ch. And moreover, sighing pervades the city, the towers sigh, the land that loved her heroes sighs; and for posterity remains the substance by reason of which, by reason of which, 172 contention came upon them whom evil destiny, and the issue of death.

Semi-Ch. In the fierceness of their hearts they divided 87 between them the possessions, so as to have an equal share; but the arbiter 173 escapes not censure from their friends, and joyless was their warfare.

Semi-Ch. Smitten by the steel, here they lie; and smitten by the steel 174 there await them—one may perchance ask what?—the inheritance of the tombs of their fathers.

Semi-Ch. From the house the piercing groan sends forth its sound loudly over them, mourning with a sorrow sufferings as o'er its own, melancholy, a foe to mirth, sincerely weeping from the very soul, which is worn down while I wail for these two princes.

Semi-Ch. We may say too of these happy men that they both wrought many mischiefs to their countrymen, and to the ranks of all the strangers, that perished in great numbers in battle.

Semi-Ch. Ill-fated was she that bare them before all women, as many as are mothers of children. Having taken to herself her own son for a husband, she brought forth these, and they have ended their existence thus by fraternal hands that dealt mutual slaughter.

Semi-Ch. Fraternal in very truth! and utterly undone were they by a severing in no wise amicable, by frenzied strife at the consummation of their feud.

Semi-Ch. But their emnity is terminated; and in the reeking earth is their life-blood mingled, and truly are they of the same blood. A bitter arbiter of strife is the stranger from beyond the sea, the whetted steel that bounded forth from the fire; and bitter is the horrible distributer of their substance, Mars, who hath brought the curse of their father truly to its consummation.

88

Semi-Ch. Hapless youths! They have obtained their portion of heaven-awarded woes, and beneath their bodies shall be a fathomless wealth of earth. 175 Alas! ye that have made your houses bloom with many troubles! And at its fall these Curses raised the shout of triumph in shrill strain, when the race had been put to flight in total rout; a trophy of Atè has been reared at the gate at which they smote each other, and, having overcome both, the demon rested.

Enter Antigone *and* Ismene .

Ant. When wounded thou didst wound again. 176

Ism. And thou, having dealt death, didst perish.

Ant. With the spear thou didst slay.

Ism. By the spear thou didst fall.

Ant. Wretched in thy deeds!

Ism. Wretched in thy sufferings!

Ant. Let tears arise.

Ism. Let groans resound.

Ant. Having slain, he shall lie prostrate. Alas! alas! my soul is maddening with sighs.

Ism. And my heart mourns within me.

Ant. Alas! thou that art worthy of all lamentation!

Ism. And thou again also utterly wretched.

Ant. By a friend didst thou fall.

Ism. And a friend didst thou slay.

Ant. Double horrors to tell of.

Ism. Double horrors to behold!

89

Ant. These horrors are near akin to such sorrows.

Ism. And we their sisters here are near to our brothers.

Ch. Alas! thou Destiny, awarder of bitterness, wretched! and thou dread shade of Œdipus! and dark Erinnys! verily art thou great in might.

Ant. Alas! alas! sufferings dismal to behold hath he shown to me after his exile.

Ant. And he returned not when he had slain him.

Ism. No—but after being saved he lost his life.

Ant. In very truth he lost it.

Ism. Ay, and he cut off his brother.

Ant. Wretched family!

Ism. That hath endured wretchedness. Woes that are wretched and of one name. Thoroughly steeped in three-fold sufferings.

Ant. Deadly to tell—

Ism. Deadly to look on.

Ch. Alas! alas! thou Destiny, awarder of bitterness, wretched! and thou dread shade of Œdipus! and dark Erinnys! verily art thou great in might.

Ant. Thou in sooth knowest this by passing through it.

Ism. And so dost thou, having learned it just as soon as he.

Ant. After that thou didst return to the city.

Ism. An antagonist too to this man here in battle-fray.

Ant. Deadly to tell.

Ism. Deadly to look on.

Ant. Alas! the trouble.

Ism. Alas! the horrors upon our family and our land, and me above all.

Ant. Alas! alas! and me, be sure, more than all.

Ism. Alas! alas! for the wretched horrors! O sovereign Eteocles, our chieftain!

Ant. Alas! ye most miserable of all men. 90

Ism. Alas! ye possessed by Atè.

Ant. Alas! alas! where in the land shall we place them both? Alas! in the spot that is most honorable. Alas! alas! a woe fit to sleep beside my father. 177

Enter Herald .

'Tis my duty to announce the good pleasure and the decree of the senators of the people of this city of Cadmus. It is resolved to bury this body of Eteocles for his attachment to his country, with the dear interment in earth! for in repelling our foes he met death in the city, and being pure in respect to the sacred rites of his country, blameless hath he fallen where 'tis glorious for the young to fall; thus, indeed, hath it been commissioned me to announce concerning this corpse: But [it has been decreed] to cast out unburied, a prey for dogs, this the corpse of his brother Polynices, inasmuch as he would have been the overturner of the land of Cadmus, if some one of the gods had not stood in opposition to his spear: and even now that he is dead, he will lie under the guilt of pollution with the gods of his country, whom he having dishonored was for taking the city by bringing against it a foreign host. So it is resolved that he, having been buried dishonorably by winged fowls, should receive his recompense, and that neither piling up by hands of the mound over his tomb should follow, nor any one honor him with shrill-voiced wailings, but that he be ungraced with a funeral at the hands of his friends. Such is the decree of the magistracy of the Cadmæans.

91

Ant. But I say to the rulers of the Cadmæans, if not another single person is willing to take part with me in burying him, I will bury him, and will expose myself 178 to peril by burying my brother. And I feel no shame at being guilty of this disobedient insubordination against the city. Powerful is the tie of the common womb from which we sprung, from a wretched mother and a hapless sire. Wherefore, my soul, do thou, willing with the willing share in his woes, with the dead, thou living, with sisterly feeling—and nought shall lean-bellied wolves tear his flesh—let no one suppose it. All woman though I be, I will contrive a tomb and a deep-dug grave for him, bearing earth in the bosom-fold of my fine linen robe, and I myself will cover him; let none imagine the contrary: an effective scheme shall aid my boldness.

Her. I bid thee not to act despite the state in this matter.

Ant. I bid thee not announce to me superfluous things.

Her. Yet stern is a people that has just escaped troubles.

Ant. Ay, call it stern 179 —yet this [corpse] shall not lie unburied.

Her. What! wilt thou honor with a tomb him whom our state abhors? 180

Ant. Heretofore he has not been honored by the gods. 181

92

Her. Not so, at least before he put this realm in jeopardy.

Ant. Having suffered injuriously he repaid with injury.

Her. Ay, but this deed of his fell on all instead of one.

Ant. Contention is the last of the gods to finish a dispute, 182 and I will bury him; make no more words.

Her. Well, take thine own way—yet I forbid thee.

[*Exit* Herald .

Ch. Alas! alas! O ye fatal Furies, proudly triumphant, and destructive to this race, ye that have ruined the family of Œdipus from its root. What will become of me? What shall I do? What can I devise? How shall I have the heart neither to bewail thee nor to escort thee to the tomb? But I dread and shrink from the terror of the citizens. Thou, at all events, shalt in sooth have many mourners; but he, wretched one, departs unsighed for, having the solitary-wailing dirge of his sister. Who will agree to this?

Sem. Let the state do or not do aught to those who bewail Polynices. We, on this side will go and join to escort his funeral procession; for both this sorrow is common to the race, and the state at different times sanctions different maxims of justice.

Sem. But we will go with this corpse, as both the city and justice join to sanction. For next to the Immortals and the might of Jove, this man prevented the city of the Cadmæans from being destroyed, and thoroughly overwhelmed by the surge of foreign enemies.

FOOTNOTES

1 Lucian, in his dialogue entitled "Prometheus," or "Caucasus," has given occasional imitations of passages in this play, not, however, sufficient to amount to a paraphrase, as Dr. Blomfield asserted. Besides, as Lucian lays the scene at Caucasus, he would rather seem to have had the "Prometheus solutus" in mind. (See Schutz, Argum.) But the ancients commonly made Caucasus the seat of the punishment of Prometheus, and, as Æschylus is not over particular in his geography, it is possible that he may be not altogether consistent with himself. Lucian makes no mention of Strength and Force, but brings in Mercury at the beginning of the dialogue. Moreover, Mercury is represented in an excellent humor, and rallies Prometheus good-naturedly upon his tortures. Thus, §6, he says, εὖ ἔχει. καταπτήσεται δὲ ἤδη καὶ ὁ ἀετὸς ἀποκερῶν τὸ ἧπαρ, ὡς πάντα ἔχοις ἀντὶ τῆς καλῆς καὶ εὐμηχάνου πλαστικῆς. In regard to the place where Prometheus was bound, the scene doubtless represented a ravine between two precipices rent from each other, with a distant prospect of some of the places mentioned in the wanderings of Io. (See Schutz, *ibid.*) But as the whole mention of Scythia is an anachronism, the less said on this point the better. Compare, however, the following remarks of Humboldt, Cosmos, vol. ii. p. 140, "The legend of Prometheus, and the unbinding of the chains of the fire-bringing Titan on the Caucasus by Hercules in journeying eastward—the ascent of Io from the valley of the Hybrites—[See Griffiths' note on v. 717, on ὑβριστὴς ποταμὸς, which *must* be a proper name]—toward the Caucasus; and the myth of Phryxus and Helle—all point to the same path on which Phœnician navigators had earlier adventured."

2 Dindorf, in his note, rightly approves the elegant reading ἄβροτον (=ἀπάνθρωπον) in lieu of the frigid ἄβατον. See Blomf. and Burges. As far as this play is concerned, the tract was not actually *impassable*, but it was so to *mortals*.

3 λεωργός=ῥᾳδιουργός, πανοῦργος, κακοῦργος. Cf. Liddell and Linwood, s. v. The interpretation and derivation of the etym. magn. ὁ τῶν ἀνθρώπων πλαστής, is justly rejected by Dindorf, who remarks that Æschylus paid no attention to the fable respecting

Prometheus being the maker of mankind.

4 The epithet παντέχνου, which might perhaps be rendered "art-full," is explained by v. 110 and 254.

5 See Jelf. Gk. Gr. §720, 2d.

6 There seems little doubt that εὐωριάζειν is the right reading. Its ironical force answers to Terence's "probe curasti."

7 I have spelled Sire in all places with a capital letter, as Jove is evidently meant. See my note on v. 49.

8 This is not a mere zeugma, but is derived from the supposition that sight was the chief of the senses, and in a manner included the rest. (Cf. Plato Tim. p. 533, C. D.) See the examples adduced by the commentators. Schrader on Musæus 5, and Boyes, Illustrations to Sept. c. Th. 98. Shakespeare has burlesqued this idea in his exquisite buffoonery, Midsummer Night's Dream, Act v. sc. 1.
Pyramus. I see a voice: now will I to the chink, To spy an I can hear my Thisby's face.

9 Claudian de rapt. Pros. II. 363. "Stellantes nox picta sinus." See on Soph. Trach. 94.

10 *I.e.*, having no rest. Soph. Œd. Col. 19. κῶλα κάμψον τοῦδ᾽ ἐπ᾽ ἀξέστου πέτρου.

11 The difficulties of this passage have been increased by no one of the commentators perceiving the evident opposition between Θεοὶ and Ζεύς. As in the formula ὦ Ζεῦ καὶ Θεοὶ (cf. Plato Protag. p. 193, E.; Aristoph. Plut. I. with Bergler's note; Julian Cæs. p. 51, 59, 76; Dionys. Hal. A. R. II. p. 80, 32-81, 20, ed. Sylb.) so, from the time of Homer downward, we find Ζεὺς constantly mentioned apart from the other gods (cf. Il. I. 423, 494), and so also with his epithet πατὴρ, as in v. 4, 17, 20, etc. (Eustath, on Il. T. I., p. 111, 30, ὅτι Ζεὺς ἀλλαχοῦ μὲν ἁπλῶς πατὴρ ἐλέχθη). There is evidently, therefore, the opposition expressed in the text: "'Tis not for the other gods (*i.e.* τοῖς ἄλλοις θεοῖς) to rule, but for Jove alone. " This view was approved, but not confirmed, by Paley.

12 See Dindorf.

13 Paley well observes that there is no objection to this interpretation, for if Prometheus could endure the daily gnawing of his entrails by the vulture, the rivets wouldn't put him to much trouble. Lucian, § 6, is content with fastening his hands to the two sides of the chasm.

14 τύχης is retained by Dindorf, but τέχνης is defended by Griffiths and Paley. I think, with Burges, that it is a gloss upon Προμηθέως.

15 So Milton, P. L. iv. 165.
Cheer'd with the grateful smell old Ocean *smiles*.
Lord Byron (opening of the Giaour):
There mildly *dimpling* Ocean's cheek Reflects the tints of many a peak, Caught by the *laughing* tides that lave Those Edens of the eastern wave.

16 Literally "filling a rod," πλήρωτος here being active. Cf. Agam. 361, ἄτης παναλώτου. Choeph. 296, παμφθάρτῳ μόρῳ. Pers. 105, πολέμους πυργοδαΐκτους. See also Blomfield, and Porson on Hes. 1117, νάρθηξ is "ferula" or "fennel-giant," the pith of which makes excellent fuel. Blomfield quotes Proclus on Hesiod, Op. 1, 52, "the νάρθηξ preserves flame excellently, having a soft pith inside, that nourishes, but can not extinguish the flame." For a strange fable connected with this theft, see Ælian Hist. An. VI. 51.

17 On the preternatural scent supposed to attend the presence of a deity, cf Eur. Hippol. 1391, with Monk's note, Virg. Æn. I. 403, and La Cerda. See also Boyes's Illustrations.

18 On δὴ cf. Jelf, Gk. Gr. § 723, 2.

19 Elmsley's reading, πέτρα . τᾷδε, is preferred by Dindorf, and seems more suitable to the passage. But if we read ταῖσδε, it will come to the same thing, retaining πέτραις.

20 Surely we should read this sentence interrogatively, as in v. 99, πῇ ποτε μόχθων Χρὴ τέρματα τῶνδ᾽ ἐπιτεῖλαι; although the editions do not agree as to that passage. So Burges.

21 Nominativus Pendens. Soph, Antig. 259, λόγοι δ᾽ ἐν ἀλλήλοισιν ἐρρόθουν κακοί, φύλαξ ἐλέγχων φύλακα, where see Wunder, and Elmsley on Eur. Heracl. 40. But it is probably only the σχῆμα καθ᾽ ὅλον καὶ μέρος, on which see Jelf, Gk. Gr. § 478, and the same thing takes place with the accusative, as in Antig. 21, sq. 561. See Erfurdt on 21.

22 See Linwood's Lexicon, s. v. ἀμείβω, whose construing I have followed.

23 Cf. Virg. Æn. I. 167, "Intus aquæ dulces, vivoque sedilia saxo."
"The rudest habitation, ye might think That it had sprung from earth self-raised, or grown Out of the living rock. "—Wordsworth's Excursion, Book vi. Compare a most picturesque description of Diana's cave, in Apul. Met. II. p. 116; Elm. Telemachus, Book I.; Undine, ch. viii.; Lane's Arabian Nights, vol. iii. p. 385.

24 Although Dindorf has left ΩΚΕΑΝΟΣ before the lines beginning with οὐ δῆτα, yet as he in his notes, p. 54, approves of the opinion of Elmsley (to which the majority of critics assent), I have continued them to Prometheus. Dindorf (after Burges) remarks that the particles οὐ δῆτα deceived the copyists, who thought that they pointed to the commencement of a new speaker's address. He quotes Soph. Œd. C. 433; Eur. Alcest. 555; Heracl. 507, sqq., where it is used as a continuation of a previous argument, as in the present passage.

25 It has been remarked that Æschylus had Pindar in mind, see Pyth. I. 31, and VIII. 20. On this fate of Enceladus cf. Philostrat. de V. Apoll. V. 6; Apollodorus I.; Hygin. Fab. 152; and for poetical descriptions, Cornel. Severus Ætna, 70, "Gurgite Trinacrio morientem Jupiter Ætna Obruit Enceladum, vasti qui pondere montis Æstuat, et patulis exspirat faucibus ignes." Virg. Æn. III. 578; Valer. Flacc. II. 24; Ovid. Met. V. Fab. V. 6; Claudian, de raptu Pros. I. 155; Orph. Arg. 1256. Strabo, I. p. 42, makes Hesiod acquainted with these eruptions. (See Goettling on Theog. 821.) But Prometheus here utters a prophecy concerning an eruption that really took place during the life of Æschylus, Ol. 75, 2, B.C. 479. Cf. Thucydides III. 116; Cluver, Sicil. Antiq. p. 104, and Dindorf's clear and learned note. There

can be little doubt but Enceladus and Typhon are only different names for the same monster. Burges has well remarked the resemblance between the Egyptian Typho and the Grecian, and considers them both as "two outward forms of one internal idea, representing the destructive principle of matter opposed to the creative." I shall refer the reader to Plutarch's entertaining treatise on Isis and Osiris; but to quote authorities from Herodotus down to the Apologetic Fathers, would be endless.

26 I think, notwithstanding the arguments of Dindorf, that ὀργῆς νοσούσης means "a mind distempered," and that λόγοι mean "arguments, reasonings." Boyes, who always shows a *poetical* appreciation of his author, aptly quotes Spenser's Fairy Queen, b. 2, c. 8, st. 26. "Words well dispost, Have secrete powre t' appease inflamed rage."
And Samson Agonistes:
"Apt words have power to swage The tumors of a troubled mind."
The reading of Plutarch, ψυχῆς appears to be a mere gloss.

27 Intellige *audaciam prudentiâ conjunctam.*—Blomfield.

28 αἰχμά is rendered "indoles" by Paley (see on Ag. 467). Linwood by "authority," which is much nearer the truth, as the spear was anciently used for the sceptre. Mr. Burges opportunely suggests Pindar's ἔγχος ζάκοτον, which he gives to Jupiter, Nem. vi. 90.

29 Asia is here personified.

30 All commentators, from the scholiast downward, are naturally surprised at this mention of Arabia, when Prometheus is occupied in describing the countries bordering on the Euxine. Burges conjectures Ἀβάριος, which he supports with considerable learning. But although the name Ἀβάριδες (mentioned by Suidas) might well be given to those who dwelt in unknown parts of the earth, from the legendary travels of Abaris with his arrow, yet the epithet ἄρειον ἄνθος seems to point to some really existing nation, while Ἀβάριες would rather seem proverbial. Till, then, we are more certain, Æschylus must still stand chargeable with geographical inconsistency.

31 I have followed Burges and Dindorf, although the latter retains ἀκαμαντοδέτοις in his text.

32 Why Dindorf should have adopted Hermann's frigid ὑποστεγάζει, is not easily seen. The reader will, however, find Griffiths' foot-note well deserving of inspection.

33 On προυσελούμενον, see Dindorf.

34 Among the mythographi discovered by Maii, and subsequently edited by Bode, the reader will find some allegorical explanations of these benefits given by Prometheus. See Myth. primus I. 1, and tertius 3, 10, 9. They are, however, little else than compilations from the commentary of Servius on Virgil, and the silly, but amusing, mythology of Fulgentius. On the endowment of speech and reason to men by Prometheus, cf. Themist. Or. xxxvi. p. 323, C. D. and xxvi. p. 338, C. ed. Hard. ; and for general illustrations, the notes of Wasse on Sallust, Cat. sub init.

35 Brick-building is first ascribed to Euryalus and Hyperbius, two brothers at Athens, by Pliny, H. N. vii. 56, quoted by Stanley. After caves, huts of beams, filled in with turf-clods, were probably the first dwellings of men. See Mallet's Northern Antiquities, p. 217, ed. Bohn. This whole passage has been imitated by Moschion apud Stob. Ecl. Phys. I. 11, while the early reformation of men has ever been a favorite theme for poets. Cf. Eurip. Suppl. 200 sqq.; Manilius I. 41, sqq.; and Bronkhus, on Tibull. I. 3, 35.

36 Cf. Apul de Deo Socr. § II. ed. meæ, "quos probe callet, qui signorum ortus et obitus comprehendit," Catullus (in a poem imitated from Callimachus) carm. 67, 1. "Omnia qui magni dispexit lumina mundi, Qui stellarum ortus comperit atque obitus." See on Agam. 7.

37 On the following discoveries consult the learned and entertaining notes of Stanley.

38 ἤγαγον φιληνίους, i.e. ὥστε φιληνίους εἶναι.

39 See the elaborate notes of Blomfield and Burges, from whence all the other commentators have derived their information. Κρᾶσις is what Scribonius Largus calls "compositio." Cf. Rhodii Lexicon Scribon, p. 364-5; Serenus Sammonicus "synthesis." The former writer observes in his preface, p. 2, "est enim hæc pars (compositio, scilicet) medicinæ ut maxime necessaria, ita certe antiquissima, et ob hoc primum celebrata atque illustrata. Siquidem verum est, antiquos herbis ac radicibus earum corporis vitia curasse."

40 Apul. de Deo Socr. § 20, ed. meæ, "ut videmus plerisque usu venire, qui nimia ominum superstitione, non suopte corde, sed alterius verbo, reguntur: et per angiporta reptantes, consilia ex alienis vocibus colligunt." Such was the voice that appeared to Socrates. See Plato Theog. p. 11. A. Xenoph. Apol. 12; Proclus in Alcib. Prim. 13, p. 41. Creuz. See also Stanley's note.

41 On these augurial terms see Abresch.

42 Although the Vatican mythologist above quoted observes of Prometheus, "deprehendit præterea rationem fulminum, et hominibus indicavit—" I should nevertheless follow Stanley and Blomfield, in understanding these words to apply to the omens derived from the flame and smoke ascending from the sacrifices.

43 Cf. Herodot. I. 91, quoted by Blomfield: τὴν πεπρωμένην μοίρην ἀδύνατά ἐστι ἀποφυγέειν καὶ τῷ θεῷ. On this Pythagorean notion of Æschylus see Stanley.

44 Or, "in pleasure at the nuptials." See Linwood. Burges: "for the one-ness of marriage."

45 No clew is given as to the form in which Io was represented on the stage. In v. 848, the promise ἐνταῦθα δή σε Ζεὺς τίθησιν ἔμφρονα does not imply any bodily change, but that Io labored under a mental delusion. Still the mythologists are against us, who agree in making her transformation complete. Perhaps she was represented with horns, like the Egyptian figures of Isis, but in other respects as a virgin, which is somewhat confirmed by v. 592, κλύεις φθέγμα τᾶς βούκερω παρθένου.

46 "Gad-fly" or "brize." See the commentators.

47 On the discrepancies of reading, see Dind. With the whole passage com-

pare Nonnus, Dionys. III. p. 62,2.
ταυροφυὴς ὅτε πόρτις ἀμειβομένοιο προσώπου εἰς ἀγέλην ἄγραυλος ἐλαύνετο σύννομος Ἰώ. καὶ δαμάλης ἄγρυπνον ἐθήκατο βουκόλον Ἥρη ποικίλον ἀπλανέεσσι κεκασμένον Ἄργον ὀπωπαῖς Ζηνὸς ὀπιπευτῆρα βοοκραίρων ὑμεναίων. Ζηνὸς ἀθητήτοιο καὶ ἐς νομὸν ἦϊε κούρη, ὀφθαλμοὺς τρομέουσα. πολυγλήνοιο νομῆος. γυιοβόρῳ δὲ μύωπι χαρασσομένη δέμας Ἰώ Ἰονίης [ἁλὸς] οἶδμα κατέγραφε φοιτάδι χηλῇ. ἦλθε καὶ εἰς Αἴγυπτον—
This writer, who constantly has the Athenian dramatists in view, pursues the narrative of Io's wanderings with an evident reference to Æschylus. See other illustrations from the poets in Stanley's notes.

48 The ghost of Argus was doubtless whimsically represented, but probably without the waste of flour that is peculiar to modern stage spectres. Perhaps, as Burges describes, "a mute in a dress resembling a peacock's tail expanded, and with a Pan's pipe slung to his side, which ever and anon he seems to sound; and with a goad in his hand, mounted at one end with a representation of a hornet or gad-fly." But this phantom, like Macbeth's dagger, is supposed to be in the mind only. With a similar idea Apuleius, Apol. p. 315, ed. Elm. invokes upon Æmilianus in the following mild terms: "At . semper obvias species mortuorum, quidquid umbrarum est usquam, quidquid lemurum, quidquid manium, quidquid larvarum oculis tuis oggerat: omnia noctium occurascula, omnia bustorum formidamina, omnia sepulchrorum terriculamenta, a quibus tamen ævo emerito haud longe abes."

49 I have followed Dindorf's elegant emendation. See his note, and Blomf. on Ag. 1.

50 After the remarks of Dindorf and Paley, it seems that the above must be the sense, whether we read ὧν with Hermann, or take ὡς for ἢ ὡς with the above mentioned editor.

51 Paley remarks that τὰς πολ. τύχας is used in the same manner as in Pers. 453, φθαρέντες="shipwrecked" (see his note), or "wandering." He renders the present passage "the adventures of her long wanderings."

52 With the earlier circumstances of this narrative compare the beautiful story of Psyche in Apuleius, Met. IV. p. 157, sqq. Elm.

53 Cf Ag. 217, ἐπεὶ δ᾽ ἀνάγκας ἔδυ λέπαδνον

54 κρήνην is the elegant conjecture of Canter, approved by Dindorf. In addition to the remarks of the commentators, the tradition preserved by Pausanias II. 15, greatly confirms this emendation. He remarks, θέρους δὲ αὖα σφίσιν ἐστὶ τὰ ῥεύματα πλὴν τῶν ἐν Λέρνῃ. It was probably somewhat proverbial.

55 I shall not attempt to enter into the much-disputed geography of Io's wanderings. So much has been said, and to so little purpose, on this perplexing subject, that to write additional notes would be only to furnish more reasons for doubting.

56 Probably the Kurban. Schutz well observes that the words οὐ ψευδώνυμον could not be applied to an epithet of the poet's own creation. Such, too, was Humboldt's idea. See my first note on this play.

57 See Schutz and Griffiths.

58 Wrapped in mystery as the liberation of Prometheus is in this drama, it may be amusing to compare the following extracts from the Short Chronicle prefixed to Sir I. Newton's Chronology.
"968. B.C. Sesak, having carried on his victories to Mount Caucasus, leaves his nephew Prometheus there, to guard the pass, etc.
"937. The Argonautic expedition. Prometheus leaves Mount Caucasus, being set at liberty by Hercules," etc.— Old Translator.

59 Stanley compares Pindar, Isth. vii. 33.
——πεπρωμένον ἦν φέρτερον γόνον [οἱ] ἄνακτα πατρὸς τεκεῖν
And Apoll. Rhod. iv. 201. Also the words of Thetis herself in Nonnus, Dionys. xxxiii. 356.
Ζεύς με πατὴρ ἐδίωκε καὶ ἤθελεν ἐς γάμον ἕλκειν, εἰ μὴ μιν ποθέοντα γέρων ἀνέκοπτε Προμηθεύς, θεσπίζων Κρονίωνος ἀρείονα παῖδα φυτεῦσαι.

60 "These were; 1. Epaphus; 2. Lybia; 3. Belus; 4. Danaus; 5. Hypermnestra; 6. Abas; 7. Prœtus; 8. Acrisius; 9. Danae; 10. Perseus; 11. Electryon; 12. Alcmena; 13. Hercules."—Blomfield.

61 For two ways of supplying the lacuna in this description of Io's travels, see Dindorf and Paley.

62 Being turned into stone. Such was the punishment of the fire-worshipers in the story of the first Lady of Baghdad. See Arabian Nights, Vol. I., p. 198. The mythico-geographical allusions in the following lines have been so fully and so learnedly illustrated, that I shall content myself with referring to the commentators.

63 See Linwood's Lexicon and Griffiths' note.

64 There is still much doubt about the elision ἔσεσθ᾽, εἰ. Others read the passage interrogatively. See Griffiths and Dindorf.

65 This pun upon the name of Epaphus is preserved by Moschus II. 50.
ἐν δ᾽ ἦν Ζεὺς, ἐπαφώμενος ἠρέμα χειρὶ θεείῃ πόρτιος Ἰναχίης. τὴν ἑπταπόρῳ παρὰ Νείλῳ ἐκ βοὸς εὐκεράοιο πάλιν μετάμειβε γυναῖκα.
and Nonnus, III. p. 62, 20:
ἔνθ᾽ Ἔπαφον Διὶ τίκτεν ἀκηρασίων ὅτι κόλπων Ἰναχίης δαμάλης ἐπαφήσατο θεῖος ἀκοίτης χερσὶν ἐρωσανέεσσι—

66 There is much difficulty in this passage. Dindorf understands ἐκείνων (Ã†gypti filiorum), and so Paley, referring to his notes on Ag. 938, Suppl. 437. Mr. Jelf, Gk. Gr., § 696, Obs. 3, appears to take the same view. There does not, therefore, seem any need of alteration. On the other interpretation sometimes given to φθόνον ἵξει σωμάτων, see Linwood, v. φθόνος.

67 σφαγαῖσι is rightly rendered "in jugulo" by Blomfield, after Ruhnk. Ep. Crit. I. p. 71. To the examples quoted add Apul. Met. I. p. 108, "per jugulum sinistrum capulotenus gladium totum ei demergit," and p. 110, "jugulo ejus vulnus dehiscit in patorem," The expression νυκτιφρουρήτῳ θράσει is well illustrated by the words of Nonnus, l. c. p. 64, 17.

καὶ κρυφίοις ξιφέεσσι σιδηροφόρων ἐπὶ λέκτρων ἄρσενα γυμνὸν Ἄρηα κατεύνασε θῆλυς Ἐνυώ.

68 See Nonnus I. c. Ovid, ep. xiv. 51, sqq.
"Sed timor, et pietas crudelibus obstitit ausis: Castaque mandatum dextra refugit opus."

69 On σφάκελος see Ruhnk. Tim. p. 123, and Blomfield.

70 See Paley. α is never intensive.

71 On this admonition, generally attributed to Pittacus, see Griffiths, and for a modern illustration in the miseries of Sir John Anvil (or Enville), Knt., the Spectator, No. 299.

72 Paley would supply πότνιαι to complete the metre.

73 I have followed Griffiths.

74 Dindorf would throw out ἄφοβος, Paley οὐ δέδια, remarking that the sense appears to require ὅτε.

75 *I.e.* possessing resources even among impossibilities. Cf. Antig. 360. ἄπορος ἐπ᾽ οὐδὲν ἔρχεται, and for the construction, Jelf, Gk. Gr. § 581, 2. obs.

76 I think Elmsley has settled the question in favor of τοῖον for οἷον.

77 "In Æschylus we seem to read the vehement language of an old servant of exploded Titanism: with him Jupiter and the Olympians are but a new dynasty, fresh and exulting, insolent and capricious, the victory just gained and yet but imperfectly secured over the mysterious and venerable beings who had preceded, TIME, HEAVEN, OCEAN, EARTH and her gigantic progeny: Jupiter is still but half the monarch of the world; his future fall is not obscurely predicted, and even while he reigns, a gloomy irresistible destiny controls his power."—Quart. Rev. xxviii, 416.

78 Uranus and Saturn. Cf. Agam. 167 sqq.

79 Milton, Samson Agon.
Dalilah. "I see thou art implacable, more deaf To prayers than winds or seas."
Merchant of Venice, Act 4, sc. 1.
"You may as well go stand upon the beach And bid the main flood bate his usual height."
See Schrader on Musæus, 320.

80 See Linwood's Lexicon. Cf. Nonnus, Dionys. II. p. 45, 22.
δεσμὰ φυγὼν δολόμητις ὁμαρτήσειε Προμηθεὺς, ἥπατος ἡβώοντος ἀφειδέα δαιτυμονῆα οὐρανίης θρασὺν ὄρνιν ἔχων πομπῆα κελεύθου.

81 I have adopted Dindorf's emendation. See his note.

82 How the cosmoramic effects here described were represented on the stage, it is difficult to say, but such descriptions are by no means rare in the poets. Compare Musæus, 314, sqq. Lucan, I. 75 sqq. and a multitude in the notes of La Cerda on Virgil, Æn. I. 107, and Barthius on Claudian. Gigant. 31, sqq. Nonnus, Dionys. I. p. 12.

83 Or, "of which may Jove the Averter be what his name imports." See Paley and Linwood's Lex.

84 This interpretation is now fully established, See Paley. Thus Cæsar, B. G. I. 29, "qui arma ferre possent: et item separatius pueri, senes;" II. 28, Eteocles wishes even the ἀχρεῖοι to assist in the common defense.

85 πιστοὶ is to be supplied with γένοισθε.

86 Although βοτὴρ may be compared with the Roman *pullarius*, yet the phrase is here probably only equivalent to δεσπότης μαντευμάτων soon after.

87 Paley prefers "nocturno concilio agitari," comparing Rhes. 88, τὰς σὰς πρὸς εὐνὰς φύλακες ἐλθόντες φόβῳ νυκτηγοροῦσι. On the authority of Griffiths, I have supplied τοὺς Ἀχαιοὺς before ἐπιβουλεύειν.

88 See my note on Prom. 863.

89 See commentators.

90 Cf. Jelf. Gk. Gr. § 566, 2.

91 See Linwood, s.v. στέφειν. Paley compares v. 267, Λάφυρα δάων δουρίπληχθ᾽ ἁγνοῖς δόμοις Στέψω πρὸ ναῶν. Adrastus alone had been promised a safe return home.

92 Cf. Eum. 515, οἶκτον οἰκτίσαιτο, *would utter cries of pity.* Suppl. 59, οἶκτον οἰκτρὸν ἀΐων, *hearing one mournful piteous cry.* The old translations rendered it, "no regret was expressed on their countenance."

93 Perhaps we might render φράξαι, *dam,* in order to keep up the metaphor of the ship. Cf. Hom. Od. V. 346, φρᾶξε δέ μιν ῥίπεσσι διαμπερὲς οἰσυΐνῃσι. The closing the ports of a vessel to keep out the water will best convey the meaning to modern readers.

94 This seems the true meaning of ἐφέστιος, *indigenous in Greece,* as Blomfield interprets, quoting Hesych, ἐφέστιος, αὐτόχθων, ἔνοικος, II. B. 125, etc. An Athenian audience, with their political jealousy of Asiatic influence, and pride of indigenous origin, would have appreciated this prayer as heartily as the one below, v. 158, πόλιν δορίπονον μὴ προδῶθ᾽ Ἑτεροφώνῳ στρατῷ, which their minds would connect with more powerful associations than the mere provincial differences of Bœotia and Argos. How great a stress was laid upon the ridicule of foreign dialect, may be seen from the reception of Pseudartabas in the Acharnians.

95 Cf. Arist. Rhet. II. 17, 6. The same sentiment, though expressed the contrary way, occurs in Eur. Troad. 26, Ἐρημία γὰρ πόλιν ὅταν λάβῃ κακή, Νοσεῖ τὰ τῶν θεῶν οὐδὲ τιμᾶσθαι θέλει.

96 The chorus survey the surrounding plains from a high part of the Acropolis of Thebes, as Antigone from the top of the palace in the Phœnissæ of Euripides, v. 103, sqq.

97 πρόδρομος=*so as to be foremost.* Cf. Soph. Antig. 108, φυγάδα πρόδρομον ὀξυτέρῳ κινήσασα χαλινῷ.

98 This passage is undoubtedly corrupt, but Dindorf's conjecture ἔλε δ᾽ ἐμὰς φρένας δέος· ὅπλων κτύπος ποτιχρίμπτεται, διὰ πέδον βοὰ ποτᾶται, βρέμει δ᾽—, although ingenious, differs too much from the *ductus literarum,* to be considered safe. Paley from the interpretation of the Medicean MS. and the reading of Robortelli, εΔΙΔεμνας, has conjectured ΔΙΑ δὲ γᾶς ἐμᾶς πεδί᾽ ὁπλοκτύπου, which seems preferable. Perhaps we might read ἐπὶ δὲ γᾶς πεδιοπλοκτύπου ὠσὶν χρίμπ. βοὰ, by tmesis, for ἐπιχρίμπτεται. Æschylus used the compound, ἐγχρίπτεσθαι, Suppl. 790, and nothing is more common than such a tmesis. I

doubt whether πεδιοπλοκτύπον is not one of Æschylus' own "high-crested" compounds. Mr. Burges has kindly suggested a parallel passage of an anonymous author, quoted by Suidas, s. v. ὑπαραττομένης · ἵππων χρεμετιζόντων, τῆς γῆς τοῖς ποσὶν αὐτῶν ὑπαραττομένης, οὔλων συγκρουομένων.

99 Cf. Soph. Antig. 106.

100 Cf. Virg. *Æn*. I. 479; "Interea ad templum non æquæ Palladis ibant Crinibus Iliades passis, peplumque ferebant Suppliciter tristes"—Statius, Theb. x. 50:

——"et ad patrias fusæ Pelopeides aras Sceptriferæ Junonis opem, reditumque suorum Exposcunt, pictasque fores, et frigida vultu Saxa terunt, parvosque docent procumbere natos * * * * * Peplum etiam dono, cujus mirabile textum," etc.

101 Here there is a gap in the metre. See Dindorf.

102 "pro vitanda servitute."—Paley.

103 Not "at the seven gates," as Valckenaer has clearly shown.

104 The paronomasia can only be kept up by rendering, "do thou, king of wolves, fall with wolf-like fierceness," etc. Müller, Dorians, vol. i. p. 325, considers that Λύκειος is connected with λύκη, *light*, not with λύκος, *a wolf*.

105 I follow Paley's emendation, αὐταῖς.

106 See a judicious note of Paley's.

107 I have borrowed Griffiths' translation. It seems impossible that ἀγνὸν τέλος could ever be a personal appeal, while σύ τε evidently shows that the address to Pallas Onca was unconnected with the preceding line. As there is probably a lacuna after Διόθεν, it is impossible to arrive at any certain meaning.

108 See Stanley. Ὄγκα is a Phœnician word, and epithet of Minerva.

109 The boys, girls, etc.

110 Cf. Eur. Hippol. 1219, sqq. καὶ δεσπότης μὲν ἱππικοῖς ἐν ἤθεσι πολὺς ξυνοικῶν ἥρπασ᾽ ἡνίας χεροῖν, ἕλκει δὲ κώπην ὥστε ναυβάτης ἀνήρ.

111 *I.e.* to adore the images placed at the head of the vessel. See Griffiths.

112 This far-fetched interpretation of an absurd text is rightly condemned by W. Dindorf in his note, who elegantly reads with Lud. Dindorf ὕδασί τ᾽ Ἰσμηνοῦ. Paley has clearly shown the origin of the corruption. Linwood is equally disinclined to support the common reading.

113 Blomfield reads ἐγὼ δέ γ᾽ ἄνδρας, the change of ΔΕΓ to ΔΕΠ being by no means a difficult one. Linwood agrees with this alteration, and Dindorf in his notes. But Paley still defends the common reading, thinking that ἐπ᾽ ἐχθροῖς is to be taken from the following line. I do not think the poet would have hazarded a construction so doubtful, that we might take ἐπὶ either with ἄνδρας, ἐχθροῖς, or by tmesis, with ἄξω.

114 The construction of the exegetical accusative is well illustrated in Jelf's Gk. Gr. § 580, 3.

115 I have followed Blomfield, and Dindorf in his notes, in reading κῦδος τοῖσδε πολίταις.

116 This is perhaps the sense required; but, with Dindorf, I can not see how it can be elicited from the common reading. Perhaps Schneider's ἀρτιτρόφοις is right, which is approved by Dindorf, Linwood, and Paley.

117 There is the same irregular antithesis between ἄλλον ἄγει and τὰ δὲ (=τᾷ δὲ) πυρφορεῖ; as in Soph. Ant. 138, εἶχε δ᾽ ἄλλα τὰ μὲν, ἄλλα δ᾽ ἐπ᾽ ἄλλοις ἐπενώμα—Ἄρης.

118 See Elmsl. on Eur. Bacch. 611. I follow Griffiths and Paley.

119 There is much difficulty in the double participle πεσὼν-κυρήσας. Dindorf would altogether omit κυρήσας, as a gloss. But surely πεσὼν was more likely to be added as a gloss, than κυρήσας. I think that the fault probably lies in πεσών.

120 This passage is scarcely satisfactory, but I have followed Paley. Perhaps if we place a comma after ὑπερτέρου, and treat ὡς ἀνδρ. δ. ὑπ. εὐτυχ. as a genitive absolute, there will be less abruptness, ἐλπίς ἐστι standing for ἐλπίζουσι, by a frequent enallage.

121 The turgidity of this metaphor is almost too much even for Æschylus!

122 The multitude of interpretations of the common reading are from their uniform absurdity sufficient to show that it is corrupt. I have chosen the least offensive, but am still certain that ἀπαρτίζει is indefensible. Hermann (who, strange to say, is followed by Wellauer) reads καταργίζει, Blomfield καταρτίζει.

123 Besides Stanley's illustrations, see Pricæus on Apul. Apol. p. 58. Pelagonius in the Geoponica, XVI. 2, observes ἀγαθοῦ δὲ ἵππου καὶ τοῦτο τεκμήριον, ὅταν ἐστηκὼς μὴ ἀνέχηται, ἀλλὰ κροτῶν τὴν γῆν ὥσπερ τρέχειν ἐπιθυμῇ. St. Macarius Hom. XXIII. 2, ἐπὰν δὲ μάθῃ (ὁ ἵππος) καὶ συνεθισθῇ εἰς τὸν πόλεμον, ὅταν ὀσφρανθῇ καὶ ἀκούσῃ φωνὴν πολέμου, αὐτὸς ἑτοίμως ἔρχεται ἐπὶ τοὺς ἐχθροὺς, ὥστε καὶ ἀπ᾽ αὐτῆς τῆς φωνῆς πτόησιν ἐμποιεῖν τοῖς πολεμίοις. Marmion, Canto V.,

"Marmion, like charger in the stall, That hears without the trumpet's call, Began to chafe and swear."

124 See Boyes' Illustrations, p. 11.

125 This seems to be the sense of μάντις ἔννοια. Blomfield would add ἔννοια to the dative, which is easier.

126 So Linwood. Justice is styled the near relation of Melanippus, because he was αἰσχρῶν ἀργὸς, v. 406. The scholiast however interprets it τὸ τῆς ξυγγενείας δίκαιον.

127 Dindorf's substitution of δικαίας for δικαίως is no improvement. Paley's δίκαιος is more elegant, but there seems little reason for alteration.

128 Probably nothing more than the lightning is meant, as Blomfield supposes. Paley quotes Eur. Cycl. 328, πέπλον κρούει, Διὸς βρονταῖσιν εἰς ἔριν κτυπῶν. And this agrees with the fate of Capaneus as described in Soph. Antig. 131, sqq.; Nonnus, XXVIII. p. 480; Eur. Phœn. 1187, sqq.

129 Blomfield compares Eur. Bacch. 733, θύρσοις διὰ χεροῖν ὡπλισμένας. But the present construction is harsher.

130 See Blomfield.

131 I follow Blomfield and Paley.

132 "We embrace this opportunity of

making a grammatical observation with respect to the older poets, which, to the best of our knowledge, has not hitherto been noticed by any grammarian or critic. Wherever a wish or a prayer is expressed, either by the single optative mood of the verb, or with μή, εἴθε, εἰ γάρ, εἴθε γάρ, the verb is in the second aorist, if it have a distinct second aorist; otherwise it may be in the present tense, but is more frequently in the first aorist."—Edinb. Rev. xix. 485.

133 *I.e.* not bearing a braggart inscription, but putting confidence in his own valor. οὐ was rightly thrown out by Erfurdt. See Paley.

134 *I.e.* from the dragon's teeth sown by Cadmus.

135 Eteoclus and the figure on his shield.

136 Like a Bacchic devotee. See Virg. Æn. IV. 301, sqq. So in the Agamemnon, v. 477.
μαρτυρεῖ δέ μοι κάσις πηλοῦ ξύνουρος, διψία κόνις, τάδε.

137 Cf. Ag. 174. Ζῆνα δέ τις ἐπινίκια κλάζων, Τεύξεται φρενῶν τὸ πᾶν. Dindorf would omit all the following lines. There is some difficulty about the sense of προσφίλεια, which I think Pauw best explains as meaning "such is the god that respectively befriends each of these champions."

138 Cf. Apollon. Rhod. I. 466, Ἴστω νῦν δόρυ θοῦρον ὅτῳ περιώσιον ἄλλων κῦδος ἐνὶ πτολέμοισιν ἀείρομαι, οὐδέ μ᾽ ὀφέλλει Ζεὺς τόσον, ὁσσάτιόν περ ἐμὸν δόρυ. Statius Theb. ix. 649—"ades o mihi dextera tantum Tu præsens bellis, et inevitable numen, Te voco, te solam superum contemptor adoro." See Cerda on Virg. Æn. X. 773.

139 So Catullus, iii. 4, 5.
Passer, deliciæ meæ puellæ, Quem plus illa oculis suis amabat.
And Vathek, p. 124 (of the English version), "Nouronihar loved her cousin more than her own beautiful eyes."—Old Translator. See Valcken. on Theocrit. xi. 53.

140 A pun upon the word παρθένος in the composition of Parthenopæus's name.

141 The figure on the shield is undoubtedly the one meant.

142 *I.e.* "he will fight by wholesale." See comm. Perhaps the English phrase to "deal a blow," to "lend a blow," is the nearest approximation to this curious idiom. Boyes quotes some neat illustrations.

143 This passage is a fair instance of the impossibility of construing certain portions of Æschylus as they are edited. Dindorf in his notes approves of Dobree's emendation, καὶ τὸν σὸν αὖτ᾽ ἀδελφοῦ ἐς πατρὸς μόρον Ἐξυπτιάζων ὄνομα, and so Paley, except that he reads ὄμμα with Schutz, and renders it "*oculo in patrio Œdipi fatum religiose sublato.*" Blomfield's προσμολὼν ὁμόσπορον seems simpler, and in better taste. ὁμόσπορον was doubtless obliterated by the gloss ἀδελφεόν (an Ionic form ill suited to the senarius), and the ὁμοιοτέλευτον caused the remainder of the error. Burges first proposed ὁμόσπορον in Troad. Append. p. 134, D. As to Paley's idea that Œdipus' death was caused "*per contentiorim filii indolem,*" I can not find either authority for the fact, or reason for its mention here, and I have therefore followed Blomfield. Dindorf's translation I can not understand. The explanations of ἐξυπτιάζων ὄνομα are amusing, and that is all.

144 *I.e.* saying Πολυνεῖκες πολυνεῖκες. Paley ingeniously remarks that ἐνδατεῖσθαι is here used in a double sense, both of *dividing* and *reproaching*. See his note, and cf. Phœn. 636. ἀληθῶς ὄνομα Πολυνείκη πατὴρ ἔθετό σοι θείᾳ, προνοίᾳ, νεικέων ἐπώνυμον.

145 See Griffiths.

146 Porson, and all the subsequent editors have bracketed this verse, as spurious, but the chief objection to this sense of καρπίζεσθαι seems to be obviated by Paley. See his note.

147 Either with πάλιν or πόλιν there is much difficulty, as without an epithet πόλις seems harshly applied to Hades. Paley thinks that τὴν μακρὰν refers both to πομπὴν and πόλιν. Dindorf adopts his usual plan when a difficulty occurs, and proposes to omit the line.

Fritzsche truly said of this learned critic, that if he had the privilege of omitting every thing he could not understand, the plays of the Grecian dramatists would speedily be reduced to a collection of fragments.

148 When the spear was not in use, it was held in the left hand, under the shield. See Blomfield.

149 Sc. king, or victor. Blomfield adopts the former.

150 This passage is not satisfactory. Paley reads ἀνδρηλατῶν, but I am doubtful about τὼς . τόνδε . τρόπον.

151 In the original there is, perhaps, a slight mixture of construction, αἵματος partly depending upon καρπός implied in πικρόκαρπον, and partly upon ἀνδροκτασίαν, ἀνδροκτ.αἵμ. being *the slaughter of a man, by which his blood is shed.*

152 Wellauer: *denuntians lucrum, quod prius erit morte posteriore*: *i.e.* victoriam quam sequetur mors. And so Griffiths and Paley.

153 Shakespeare uses this name in the opening speech of King Henry, in part I. :
No more the thirsty Erinnys of this soil Shall daub her lips with her own children's blood.
Old Translator.

154 See above, v. 383.

155 Somewhat to the same effect is the dream of Atossa in the Persæ.

156 I prefer Blomfield's transposition to Dindorf's correction, βλαψιφρόνως, which, though repudiated in the notes, is still adopted by Paley.

157 A noble impersonation of the sword.

158 Shakespeare, King John, Act 4, sc. 2:
That blood, which own'd the breadth of all this isle, Three foot of it doth hold. King Henry IV. part I. Act 5, sc. 5:
Fare thee well, great heart! Ill-weav'd ambition, how much art thou shrunk! When that this body did contain a spirit, A kingdom for it was too small a bound; But now, two paces of the vilest earth Is room enough.

159 Surely the full stop after πόλιν in v. 749 should be removed, and a colon, or mark of hyperbaton substituted. On

looking at Paley's edition, I find myself anticipated.

160 This is Griffiths' version of this awkward passage. I should prefer reading ἀλκὰν with Paley, from one MS. So also Burges.

161 See my note on Soph. Philoct. 708, ed. Bohn.

162 This seems the best way of rendering the bold periphrase, ὁ πολύβοτος αἰὼν βροτῶν. See Griffiths.

163 I follow Paley. Dindorf, in his notes, agrees in reading τροφᾶς, but the metre seems to require ἐπίκοτος. Griffiths defends the common reading, but against the ancient authority of the schol. on Œd. Col. 1375. See Blomfield.

164 Blomfield with reason thinks that a verse has been lost.

165 The care which the Messenger takes to show the bright side of the picture first, reminds us of Northumberland's speech, Shakespeare, King Henry IV. part II. Act 1, sc. 1:
This thou would'st say—Your son did thus and thus; Your brother, thus; so fought the noble Douglas; Stopping my greedy ear with their bold deeds; But in the end, to stop mine ear indeed, Thou hast a sigh to blow away this praise, Ending with—brother, son, and all are dead.
— Old Transl.

166 This is a good example of the figure chiasmus, the force of which I have expressed by the bracketed words repeated from the two infinities. See Latin examples in the notes of Arntzenius on Mamertin. Geneth. 8, p. 27; Pang. Vett. t. i.

167 The Messenger retires to dress for the Herald's part.
Horace's rule, "Nec quarta loqui persona laboret," seems to have been drawn from the practice of the Greek stage. Only three actors were allowed to each of the competitor-dramatists, and these were assigned to them by lot. (Hesychius, Νέμησις ὑποκριτῶν.) Thus, for instance, as is remarked by a writer in the Quarterly Review, in the Œdipus at Colonus, v. 509, Ismene goes to offer sacrifice, and, after about forty lines, returns in the character of Theseus. Soon afterward, v. 847, Antigone is carried off by Creon's attendants, and returns as Theseus after about the same interval as before.— Old Translation. The translator had misquoted the gloss of Hesychius.

168 This is the tragic account. See Soph. Antig. 170, sqq.; Eurip. Phæn. 757, sqq. But other authors mention descendants of both.

169 Another pun on Πολυνείκης.

170 Cf. Romeo and Juliet, Act 4, sec. 3:
"I have a faint cold fear thrills through my veins."

171 This passage is confessedly corrupt. Paley seems to have rightly restored ἄστολον from the ἄστολον θεωρίδα in Robertelli's edition. This ship, as he remarks, would truly be ἄστολος, in opposition to the one sent to Delphi, which was properly said στέλλεσθαι ἐπὶ θεωρίαν. The words ἀστιβῆ Ἀπόλλωνι confirm this opinion. In regard to the allusions, see Stanley and Blomfield, also Wyttenbach on Plato Phædon. sub. init.

172 This repetition of δι᾿ ὧν is not altogether otiose. Their contention for estate was the cause both of their being αἰνόμοροι and of the νεῖκος that ensued.

173 *I.e.* the sword. Cf. v. 885.

174 This epithet applied to their ancestral tombs doubtless alludes to the violent deaths of Laïus and Œdipus.

175 On the enallage σώματι for σώμασι see Griffiths. The poet means to say that this will be all their possession after death. Still Blomfield's reading, χώματι, seems more elegant and satisfactory.

176 Pauw remarks that Polynices is the chief subject of Antigone's mourning, while Ismene bewails Eteocles. This may illustrate much of the following dialogue, as well as explain whence Sophocles derived his master-piece of character, the Theban martyr-heroine, Antigone.

177 Throughout this scene I have followed Dindorf's text, although many improvements have been made in the disposition of the dramatis personæ. Every one will confess that the length of ἰὼ ἰὼ commonplaces in this scene would be much against the play, but for the animated conclusion, a conclusion, however, that must lose all its finest interest to the reader who is unacquainted with the Antigone of Sophocles!

178 Wellauer (not Scholfield, as Griffiths says) defends the common reading from Herodot. V. 49.

179 τράχυνε But T. Burgess' emendation τραχύς γε seems better, and is approved by Blomfield.

180 Soph. Ant. 44. ἦ γὰρ νοεῖς θάπτειν σφ᾿ ἀπόρρητον πόλει.

181 I have taken Griffiths' translation of what Dindorf rightly calls "lectio vitiosa," and of stuff that no sane person can believe came from the hand of Æschylus. Paley, who has often seen the truth where all others have failed, ingeniously supposes that οὐ is a mistaken insertion, and, omitting it, takes διατετίμηται in this sense: "*jam hic non amplius a diis honoratur; ergo ego eum honorabo.*" See his highly satisfactory note, to which I will only add that the reasoning of the Antigone of Sophocles, vss. 515, sqq. gives ample confirmation to his view of this passage.

182 Blomfield would either omit this verse, or assign it to the chorus.

93

The Hamilton, Locke and Clark SERIES OF Interlinear Translations
Have long been the Standard and are now the *Best Translated* and *Most Complete* Series of Interlinears published.
12mo., well bound in Half Leather. Price reduced to $1.50 each. Postpaid to any address.
Latin Interlinear Translations:
VIRGIL—By Hart and Osborne .
HORACE—By Stirling, Nuttall and Clark .
CICERO—By Hamilton and Clark .
SALLUST—By Hamilton and Clark .
OVID—By George W. Heilig .
JUVENAL—By Hamilton and Clark .

LIVY—By Hamilton and Clark.
CORNELIUS NEPOS—By Hamilton and Underwood.
Greek Interlinear Translations:
HOMER'S ILIAD—By Thomas Clark.
XENOPHON'S ANABASIS—By Hamilton and Clark.
GOSPEL OF ST. JOHN—By George W. Heilig.

S. Austin Allibone, the distinguished author, writes:
"There is a growing disapprobation, both in Great Britain and America, of the disproportionate length of time devoted by the youthful student to the acquisition of the dead languages; and therefore nothing will tend so effectually to the preservation of the Greek and Latin grammars as their judicious union (the fruit of an intelligent compromise) with the Interlinear Classics."
DAVID McKAY, Publisher, Philadelphia.
Formerly published by Charles De Silver & Sons.